A
VIRAGO
KEEPSAKE

to celebrate

TWENTY
YEARS

of publishing

Published by VIRAGO PRESS Limited, 1993
20–23 Mandela Street, Camden Town, London NW1 0HQ

A CIP *catalogue record for this book is available from the
British Library*

Typeset by The Electronic Book Factory Ltd, Fife, Scotland
Printed in England by Cox & Wyman Ltd, Reading, Berks,
on TAMCREAMY Bulky Mechanical Paper
made in Finland by ANJALA MILL
and supplied by LAMCO PAPER SALES LIMITED

Acknowledgements

Acknowledgements are due to the following for permission to include their work in the Keepsake: 'Recovery from Self-Betrayal', Afterword to *More Revealed* by Ken Ragge, © Alice Miller 1993; 'Meditations on a Human Sacrifice' from *The Basement* by Kate Millett, Copyright © 1990 by Kate Millett; 'The Real Hillary Factor' © by Deborah Tannen/NYT OpEd, distributed by New York Times Syndication Sales; 'A Short Tour of the Russian Asylum' by Tatyana Tolstaya © the Guardian; 'Angela Carter: Heroic Optimism, Fantastic Flights' from the Introduction to *The Second Virago Book of Fairy Tales* © Marina Warner 1992.

CONTENTS

INTRODUCTION

For this birthday, we wanted to produce something really special. Something which would mark the twenty years of our existence and share the pride we take in the achievements of our publishing house. Thanks to our authors we have this Keepsake, which does exactly that, and it is my very great pleasure to thank the twenty authors who created it – for their generosity in making time to write at all and for the excellence of their writing.

I hope that everyone who reads the Keepsake will enjoy it even half as much as we have. The pleasure it has given us shows how, in putting together something to give away, we have ourselves been given a present: a reflection of Virago which reveals our ideals, our practice and our books at their best.

Thanks must go to not only these women but to all our authors for the books they entrust to us. Unsurprisingly, the only unpleasant task connected with the Keepsake was that of reducing the list of contributors to just twenty.

As with all publishers, books are our lifeblood, but at Virago, what we see as being of equal importance is the existence of the Press itself. We have always worked to be greater than the sum of our parts. We want to show what women can do when they put their minds to it and these essays give a wonderful picture of what Virago has been and will be.

While pride of place is given to women's writing and issues – they are obviously central to everything we do – feminism at Virago has by intention taken many guises. It underlies the diversity and inclusiveness of the list, the passionate concern to publish the best, and the belief that women's writing and issues could be the foundation of an inspirational, financially viable list. We have published across many disciplines and in each, taking the woman's part has brought us to the very heart of the matter. Women may not yet have equal power or influence, but we certainly have the talent.

Those talents have provided us with the six hundred titles we currently have in print and the hundred new titles and re-issues we publish each year. They have enabled us publish the voices of women from all over the world, women who recall their lives with devastating intensity, women who tell stories, create fictions and conjure up images of extraordinary power, and women who make us laugh. We publish the work of writers with the all-important ability to find ways of looking at things differently, to make new connections and provide unexpected insights. These are revealed in novels and poetry; in the exciting juxtaposition of poems or stories in an anthology; in a critique of some unexamined aspect of our culture; in an unputdownable thriller, a revealing biography or a work of illuminating literary criticism.

These books have been published by a company which itself demonstrates the virtues of diversity and difference. There were the early days, referred to in several of the Keepsake pieces, when two women of genuinely outstanding ability – Carmen Callil whose idea it was to start a feminist publishing house and whose unrivalled energy got things moving, and Ursula Owen who brought her myriad connections and tremendous experience as an editor – worked from a dining room table in Chelsea. Nearly ten years of intense, almost frenetic activity followed, and saw rapid growth in both our turnover and reputation. It was also during these years that the size of the staff grew, and we were joined by several women who stayed to play a central role in the life of the company: Lennie Goodings, now Publisher, whose early talent for publicity is revealed in Margaret Atwood's Keepsake story; Lynn Knight who now both commissions and runs the Virago Modern Classics list; Ruth Petrie who joined us from *Spare Rib* and is now Senior Editorial Director.

In 1982 a new and very different era began, when Virago became part of the Chatto Bodley Head and Cape Group. During a five-year period the company gained much from the association with those long-established publishers, but during 1986 we realised that the likelihood of the Group being taken over was so great that it was time to try and buy back the company and take full control of our destiny again. This was achieved at the end of 1987 by means of a management buy-out, just as the other publishers in the Group were bought by Random House US.

So, after only five years of life as that increasingly rare breed, the medium-sized independent publisher, we can look back on twenty fascinating and enjoyable years and celebrate the creativity, skill and dedication of the women, and men, who have participated in our publishing. It is our privilege to have worked with them for twenty years and we take this opportunity to thank them.

And if the Keepsake conveys even in part our experience of the extraordinary times we have had it will have succeeded. There has been fun, excitement and shared ideals underpinned by hard work and loyalty: hard work and commitment from the women who have worked at Virago over the years, and loyalty from both them and all of you who buy our books. Your appreciation, concern and criticisms of our endeavours make the world of difference, and who knows, perhaps even a difference to the world.

Here's to all of us and more than another twenty years of successful publishing.

Harriet Spicer, Managing Director
January 1993

MAYA ANGELOU

born in St Louis, Missouri in 1928, has been waitress, singer, actor, dancer, editor, and is now writer, poet and Reynolds Professor of American Studies at Wake Forest University, North Carolina. Her 'roller-coaster life' began with a childhood of loss, poverty and abuse. After touring Europe and Africa in *Porgy and Bess* she became involved in the Black struggles of the 1960s, then edited *African Review* in Ghana for several years. *I Know Why the Caged Bird Sings*, the first of her highly acclaimed five-volume autobiographical sequence first appeared in 1969. All these books together with her collections of poetry, are published by Virago.

In January 1993 Professor Angelou had the signal honour of reading her specially commissioned poem, 'On the Pulse of Morning' at the Inauguration Ceremony of Bill Clinton – the first poet to receive this honour since Robert Frost, who appeared at the Inauguration of J.F. Kennedy in 1960. Virago published the text of this poem in Spring 1993.

WORDS AND MORE WORDS
by MAYA ANGELOU

Words. Words. I have always loved them. I love
words spoken and I love words sung, and I
even love to see words sitting primly on pages.
However they arrive in my mind – auricularly or optically
– they come welcomed and heralded. It was fitting that I
would become a writer.

'You have done so many things in your life. Today, how
would you describe yourself?' The interviewer always
asks the question, presuming no one has ever before
formulated such enquiry. Without hesitation I reply, 'I
am a writer.' The strength of my conviction can be heard
in the brevity of my response, 'I am a writer.' Hence,
direct, even a little brusque. Almost 'How could you dare
ask such a vapid question? Everyone knows I am a writer.
Why are you one of the two or three literate persons in
the world who doesn't already know the answer to that
question?'

There are a number of reasons for believing myself to
be a writer. I have had eleven books published. Some have
been bestsellers. I have written and produced screenplays,
stage plays and television scripts. Poetry, even journalistic
accounts of current events have been printed.

I do realise that every human being in the world who
is not mute, in solitary confinement or a hermit by choice

uses words to communicate with other humans, and that as a writer I must use those same tools (words), used so casually or pointedly by everyone else, in order to make an old thing seem new, a stale idea fresh. I am made a little intimidated by that knowledge, yet I persist in describing myself as a writer. As a writer I know that I must select studiously the nouns, pronouns, verbs, adverbs, etcetera, and by a careful syntactical arrangement make readers laugh, reflect or riot. Knowing the difficulties which face the writer, I still introduce myself to everyone, including my mirror, with these words 'I am a writer.'

I hold steadily, resolutely to the statement until the time comes when I must be what I claim to be. Then I sit down to face the legal-size yellow pad upon which I am forced to prove myself and taking my pen in hand, start quaking before I can put the first words down.

My too good memory serves me ill on those occasions. I remember the quotes of Edna St Vincent Millay, 'I shall die, but that is all I will do for death.' I think of the spirit-rousing call of James Weldon Johnson, 'Lift ev'ry voice and sing, till earth and heaven ring.' Keats's lyricism, 'A thing of beauty is a joy for ever,' nearly makes me drop my pen. Langston Hughes's historical memory, 'I've known rivers deep as the flow of human blood in human veins', bewitch my writing hand. I am forced to place the pen upon the yellow pad and allow the great writers of the past to enter into my writing room. Shelley shoulders Gwendolyn Brooks. Gerard Manley Hopkins walks side by side with Amiri Baraka. Paule Marshall and André Gide parade their poesy and prose; then, finally satisfied with their shadowy pavane, they leave me and I begin to write. The first words (of course to be deleted) from each book, poem, essay or short story I have ever written are 'Please God, let me be a writer.'

MARGARET ATWOOD

born in Ottawa in 1939, spent much of her early life in the northern Ontario and Quebec bush country and started writing at the age of five. Educated at the University of Toronto and Radcliffe, she published her first, prize-winning, volume of poetry in 1966, and is a distinguished poet. *The Edible Woman*, the first of her seven novels so far (all published by Virago), appeared in 1969. *The Handmaid's Tale* (1985) won the Arthur C. Clarke Award for Science Fiction and the Governor-General's Award, was shortlisted for the Booker Prize and made into a major film. *Cat's Eye*, her most recent novel, was also shortlisted for the Booker Prize, and *Good Bones*, a sparkling collection of occasional pieces, is published by Virago in 1993.

DUMP BINS AND SHELF STRIPS
by MARGARET ATWOOD

The first book of mine that Virago published was *Surfacing*. In England, then, being Canadian was sort of like being cross-eyed, only less interesting: most people would gamely pretend not to notice, or throw you a look of pity and then swiftly escape to talk to someone else. So it was refreshing to get a letter from an English outfit I'd never heard of that wanted to reprint my second novel. It was a good letter, too. In addition to its request, it explained Virago's outlook and publishing policy – books by and about women, but in all areas and from many periods and points of view. The list of editorial consultants was, as the young were soon to say, awesome. We linked forces.

That was in the mid-seventies, when Virago occupied a single room in a crumbling building on one of the grubbier streets in Soho. You walked up several flights of none-too-clean stairs to get to it, past an establishment which was – I think – a hairdresser's, but which sticks in my mind as a massage parlour. Certainly there were a lot of men in raincoats hanging around. I prepared ripostes, in case of sudden stairway unbuttonings – 'Listen pal, where I come from we put toothpicks through those and serve them on soda crackers' – but I never had to use them. Maybe my own raincoat was daunting; or maybe the wind of Virago's name had already gone round about it.

Once you reached the publishing company itself you could scarcely move for books, because all functions, including warehousing and shipping, were carried out in the same place. At the time there were only four Viragoites – as in stalactites or happy Vegemites; or Viragoesses, as in poetesses or ogresses; or Viragoettes, as in drum majorettes, vedettes or Smurfettes; or perhaps *Viragoes* would be correct, as in *vir* and *virago*, which would give us *waiter* and *waitrago* – anyway, there were four of them, crammed in among the books. It felt like home to me, as many Canadian writers of my generation had been involved in similarly crowded small publishing ventures, having had to start them because of scarcity in the home territories. Carmen Callil was the chief (Chiefago?) then; I liked her immediately, because she was shorter than me (few are) but didn't let it cramp her style any. Also she was a wild colonial girl, like me, only wilder. In her hands, the Old School Tie publishing network was about to become macramé.

Several other publishing ventures had been started at about the same time as Virago; most were failing. I asked Carmen the secret of her success. Well, she said, those other people were – er – men. They were used to having rooms of their own, and secretaries to do the routine jobs for them, but secretaries cost extra money, which Virago did not at the moment have. 'Here,' she said, 'we lick our own stamps.' A gluey-tongued self-sticker from way back, I was impressed.

Some years later, Virago had licked itself into a different and more commodious address and some secretarial assistance, and was about to publish the paperback of *Bodily Harm*. They tried something quite daring and potentially disastrous – a large print run, their first. This involved me with Lennie Goodings, then the Publicity

7

Director, and questions neither of us had faced before. 'Do you know what a dump bin is?' she asked. 'What about a shelf strip?' We soon found out.

Many shelf strips and dump bins later, Virago published the paperback version of my novel, *Cat's Eye*. Their dump bin – which, should you not know, is that boxy stand thing you see in bookstores, with oblong compartments full of books and some sort of slogan or picture on the top – was a triumph: it was in the shape of the black-clad veiled woman on the book's cover, and the compartments for the books themselves were in the area of her stomach. This figure required a taxi all to itself when it was taken to a trade fair, and several Viragoes reported having had nightmares about it. I forgot to ask whether the nightmare included a stomachful of unsold books, or was just the figure itself.

Probably the latter, because by this time Virago had achieved a rare status: Brand Name Recognition. I have a habit of lurking about in bookstores, which dates from the time when I actually sold books (by hand, as they say) to such establishments. So I lurked about in British bookstores, and I would hear people say: *Got any new Viragos?* Mostly, as publishers are never tired of telling you when parachuting you behind the lines or convincing you to go on talk shows, the author *is* the brand name. You keep looking on your body for tiny logo stickers, or CAIN in red on your forehead. But for these readers, the word *Virago* in itself seemed enough to guarantee a certain level of quality.

It's a great tribute to the taste and acumen of the Virago group that this should be so. In a mere twenty years Virago has made itself into a noun. In publishing, this is very rare. So is Virago, in the 1483 sense of the word – 'remarkably good and fine'.

Happy Birthday to Virago, and to all the Viragoites. Long may your shelf strips wave!

NINA BAWDEN

a Fellow of the Royal Society of Literature, is admired as a writer who unravels the emotions that simmer beneath respectable family life. She was born in London, where she still lives, and educated at Oxford. Her first novel appeared in 1953. Since then she has published a further nineteen adult novels, together with many acclaimed children's books. Nina Bawden won the *Yorkshire Post* Novel of the Year Award with *Afternoon of a Good Woman* (1976) and was shortlisted for the 1987 Booker Prize with *Circles of Deceit* (later a BBC film). Her latest novel, *Family Money* (1991), is published by Virago, as are five of her earlier works. *The Ice House* and *A Grain of Truth* will both be published by Virago in 1993.

CODED AUTOBIOGRAPHY

by NINA BAWDEN

Until recently, when a book was finished – published, that is, not in manuscript – my real relationship with it was over. Interested as I am in its future, its reception, its sales, it is only as I would be interested in the career of a young relation who gratifyingly, and sometimes unexpectedly, sends money home. The total immersion in the story that I felt while I was writing, my close association with the characters whom I often seemed to know more about – and certainly understood more – than the 'real' people about me, had gone. (Which is just as well, perhaps: it would be tedious to have the people from one book cluttering up the next one, a little like unwanted relations from a previous marriage spoiling a wedding party.)

Lately, however, I have discovered that I have not 'lost' these people as completely as I had imagined. I had always known that the characters in my children's novels had not disappeared in quite the same way as the characters in the stories for adults, presumably because I occasionally read aloud both to children and to people interested in children's literature, and in doing so reminded myself of this or that fictional person who had once been not just close to me but part of myself as a writer's characters usually are.

Now, since Virago have begun reissuing those of my novels that are out of print, and I have been looking at them afresh in their beautiful new jackets and even (out of anxiety as much as vanity) been glancing through them, re-reading here and there, I have realised not just that the characters in them are still in my mind – *lurking* there ever since I first got to know them, keeping quiet and out of the way in some unvisited attic – but that I still know as much about them as I ever did. Indeed, if the (ineffably tedious to my mind) idea of my writing a sequel to one of my novels should ever occur to a publisher with a very long purse, I could oblige without difficulty.

The second thing that I realised, daring to look at my work as a whole and to take it as seriously as I would take the work of another writer unknown to me, was that it reflected the concerns of my adult life, including to some extent what a sociologist might call the rise and fall of the welfare state. The doctor-stepfather in *A Little Love, a Little Learning*, and the submerged but battling heroine of *A Woman of My Age* who deceives her husband, not because she has a lover, but because she is attending a Labour Party meeting, both assume that the value of public services is accepted by all good people without any question. The parents in *The Birds on the Trees*, who have a son expelled from school for taking drugs in the sixties, are finding out that the cradle-to-grave safety net has large holes in it. The travel agent in *George Beneath a Paper Moon* makes a fortune by being in at the beginning of the package deal boom in the seventies. And *Family Money*, a story about families, old age, greed and money, is set at the end of the disastrous Thatcher decade when productive work was dismissed, service industries encouraged, and the rise in property values seemed the quickest way to make money.

The third discovery, the most interesting to me, was

that *all* my novels, including the children's books, if read in sequence would provide (would provide for me, at any rate) a kind of coded autobiography. It is not that I have always written about myself, although of course all writers write about themselves to some extent, just that everywhere, slipped in – sometimes without my noticing it until after the book was published – there is something discussed or commented on that was of passionate interest to me at the time. There is a legal case in *Afternoon of a Good Woman* which is very like a case that I had sat on in the Crown Court, the injustice of the outcome of which had shocked me more deeply than any other I witnessed in my years as a magistrate. A man was convicted by a stupid jury for no reason other than muddle and incompetence on the part of his defending counsel. And in *Circles of Deceit*, playing a minor role, there is a schizophrenic boy, very like my older son, whom I had never intended to include in the novel. He crept in, it seemed, while my back was turned, and became part of the plot.

I mention this personal sadness in order to make a last point. A writer's work may be a coded autobiography but only a very close friend could decipher it and write a true account. My son was already dead when I wrote *Circles of Deceit*, and it would have suited the story if the character who was based on him had died at the end of the book. But I couldn't bear to kill him off, out of tenderness, and so I managed to save him until the last page was written, even though I hinted that he would not last long. And I believe that to keep him alive made a more effective ending.

All writers are liars. They twist events to suit themselves. They make use of their own tragedies to make a better story. They batten on their relations. They are terrible people. They 'put people in books' – although by the time the book is under way they are honestly convinced that the character they are writing about has sprung entirely from their imagination. Writers are not to be trusted. Except in one thing. Most of us try to do our best for the sake of the story and try to be true, not to ourselves because that would be a hopeless task, but to the book we are writing.

WILLA CATHER

(1873–1947), one of America's foremost twentieth-century writers, was born in Virginia where her ancestors had farmed for generations. In 1901 the family moved to Nebraska, then frontier territory. She graduated from the University of Nebraska to become a teacher and journalist before taking up writing full time in 1912. Of her many books Virago publishes *Alexander's Bridge*, her first novel, *O Pioneers!*, *The Song of the Lark*, *My Antonia*, *One of Ours*, *A Lost Lady*, *The Professor's House*, *My Mortal Enemy*, *Death Comes for the Archbishop*, *Lucy Gayheart*, *Sapphira and the Slave Girl* and *The Short Stories of Willa Cather*.

A.S. Byatt is an acclaimed novelist and a distinguished scholar and critic. Her novel *Possession* won the 1991 Booker Prize.

WILLA CATHER
by A.S. BYATT

I discovered Willa Cather through writing the Virago prefaces from 1979 onwards. She was not part of my childhood or student reading, or even of the American literature courses I had taught at London University. I became intrigued by her after reading Ellen Moers's account of her work in *Literary Women*, and when Carmen Callil persuaded Alfred Knopf, who held the copyrights, that Virago was a respectable and honourable enough house to publish her, I read all her books, and wrote prefaces to nine of them. I only came slowly to see that she was a major writer during this time. It takes a long time to feel one's way into her strange pace and shifts of focus, which I now think were radically innovative, and are still not wholly understood by critics – but have the disadvantage of looking, at a cursory glance, as though they were *simply* pastoral tales, or novels of morals and manners.

They are both these things, of course. She took a new subject matter – the settling of the Midwest of the United States by Eastern Europeans, the meeting of American earth – wintry Nebraska, burning New Mexico, cold rocky Quebec – and old civilisations, French, German, Polish. She also wrote tales of sexual betrayal, flaring violence, brooding passion, which have been compared to

Henry James and Edith Wharton but have a kind of bare, almost impersonal quality also akin to myth and folk tale. She wrote about fierce female ambition – notably in *The Song of the Lark* – and also about fierce resignation in the face of death and dissolution.

I was interested in all these things as a scholar and a reader. I was interested in the way she managed to combine an extremely sophisticated and lively response to European culture – Virgil, Wagner, Thomas Mann, Flaubert – with descriptions of the immediate physical privations and pleasures of the world of the pioneers, the missionaries, the farmers and explorers. Something in her spoke to something in me when she wrote of the way in which civilisation clings tenaciously to life in harsh circumstances. Civilisation to Cather is a human artefact made up of many things, from the very simple – a well-made soup with good bread, a pot of parsley kept alive to add savour to good French food in a Canadian winter – to the very complex – a woman from the Midwest learning how to sing Wagner's Fricka from her own mother's experience, the building of a beautiful cathedral out of alien stone. Civilisation is fragile and enduring – in *The Song of the Lark* the singer's throat and the ancient Indians' perfectly crafted pots are both vessels that contain it. Cather compared her own artistic ambitions to those of the seventeenth-century Dutch painters who recorded lovingly the details of daily life – walls and glass panes, jugs and dishes, dresses and furnishings – and also showed open windows through which could be seen the space of rushing grey seas and ships.

I came to love her for her complex depiction and care for these things. But what the writer in me responded to is harder to describe and still more important. It is to do with the real complexity and variety of the pace of her apparently calm, even statuesque writing, and with the way in which this relates to the very basic human rhythms of a whole life and death.

I think she partly learned this from George Eliot, whom she admired greatly, though I am guessing about this, and I think she also learned it because she knew a great deal about how human beings make images of their worlds in music and paintings, too, and the very different rhythms of these forms. When I first came to grips with George Eliot I kept saying to myself, 'It is all about *uses of energy*' – a feminist problem, the problem of powerful women reined in and inactive, the problem of passion boiling and blocked off (Maggie Tulliver, Dorothea), the problem of inertia (Casaubon, Bulstrode's fear, Gwendolen's fear, Grandcourt's menace). Cather's long rhythms are to do with human energy too, but are not so much attached to individual struggles and defeats. A landmark in my attachment to Cather was when I read her friend E. S. Sergeant's account of her discovery of her 'own' style, in *O Pioneers!*

When I let her know that the only flaw I could find in *O Pioneers!* was that it had no sharp skeleton she swiftly replied, true enough, I had named a weakness. But the land has no sculptured lines or features. The soil is soft, light, fluent, black, for the grass of the plains creates this type of soil as it decays. This influences the mind and memory of the author and so the composition of the story.

What can be felt in a Cather novel is a form created out of this sense of fluidity, memory, life and decay. Her people rise and grow like trees in landscapes and everything changes at different paces, fast and furiously in the young and passionate, quietly in the old and defeated, slower still in whole civilisations, and slower still on the face of the earth. You can at times, in a Cather novel, *feel* both the blood pulsing angrily, and the breath exhaling slowly, and plants growing, and the earth turning, and your own consciousness held in all these rhythms at once, in the apparently artless and random pace of Cather's prose. It is a gift akin to perfect pace in music, Cather's sense of narrative rhythm and her use of it is her unique genius. Once one's ear – or body – is alerted to it, one can read at different paces within the movement of a whole text, taking pleasure in sharp shocks and long blasts of wind, in hot stillnesses and mute miseries, in the eternity of a bowl of Venetian glass fruit in a cold castle in seventeenth-century Quebec, or the bloody blast of murder in a spring orchard in *O Pioneers!*

AMANDA CROSS

is the pen-name of Carolyn Heilbrun, Avalon Professor in the Humanities at Columbia University, New York. Educated at Wellesley and Columbia, she has held several teaching posts and fellowships. Under her real name she has published a number of scholarly studies, and began writing feminist detective stories as Amanda Cross in 1964. The first of these, *In the Last Analysis*, was nominated for Best First Novel by the Mystery Writers of America. This, and her nine succeeding novels, of which the most recent is *The Players Come Again*, are all published by Virago.

AMBIVALENCE, THY NAME IS WOMAN

by CAROLYN HEILBRUN (AMANDA CROSS)

When Kate Fansler first appeared in 1964, she was the only female detective in print in the United States. Looking back upon her salad days, I find that she, like Cleopatra, was green in judgement, cold in blood. I, however, thought she was pretty daring and special at the time, and perhaps she was. But she didn't bond with other women, she didn't see through Freud, and she was far too willowy and elegant. I was thirty-eight and she was thirty, more or less. (She has aged, but not with the relentlessness required of us mortals; she is now – or will be, the next time she turns up in print – around fifty-five.)

In the years since her first appearance, she has been followed by a wealth of female detectives and I greet them joyfully, although there are more than I can well name. The pleasure they bring me is like that of a lonely immigrant eventually finding herself the oldest at a family gathering of astonishing size and range. Some younger family members will inevitably be just a little ashamed of her or, at any event, impatient. But how do I feel today about this family of women detectives and women crime writers?

I feel, first, marvellous and then intrigued. Women detectives, like sensible women professionals in all fields, have learned what they could from the men, but have dropped the macho, arrogant, unambivalent self-satisfaction. Ambivalence, thy name is woman, and thanks be for that. In the US we have Sara Paretsky's V.I. Warshawski, honoured by the British Crime Writers Association but not (characteristically) by America's Mystery Writers' Association. We have, in addition, policewomen, medical examiners, lawyers and others more or less licensed to pursue crime. Women detectives who used to be amateurs have become professionals, thus moving from the English influence on women crime writers (which can scarcely be overestimated) to the American model of the private eye. Kate is still an amateur, but at least she gets called in on cases she might be able to unravel; she does not, like American TV's Angela Lansbury character, trip over a corpse every time she ventures beyond her doorstep, and sometimes without even going out. Kate Fansler has her standards, and, beyond detection, a life to live.

I am also intrigued by the tendency of most women detectives to relate their adventures in the first person. We are in their minds, we struggle with them, just as we did with Sam Spade and Philip Marlowe and their American progeny. Earlier English women writers like Sayers used the third person, and Kate followed in their wake. But, unlike many other writers in the third person, I have never become, in the Dickens mode, an 'omniscient author'. P.D. James moves from the mind of one character to another, and I find, ardent admirer though I am of James and all her works, that I long to stay inside the minds of Adam Dalgliesh and James's two wonderful young women detectives, Cordelia Gray, private eye, and Kate Miskin, police inspector. I don't want to be in the mind of the murderer, and I'd rather the other characters told their stories, as Sayers's characters did, to the detectives and not directly to me. This is an idiosyncratic opinion on my part, and should be noted concomitantly with the fact that P.D. James sells more books in a week than I do in a year, and is a fine writer besides.

I rejoice, not only in the number of women detectives whose adventures we may joyfully choose among, but also at the change in male detectives and their creators, where such changes have occurred. Women crime writers are creating admirable men, and some men are also creating male characters who are terrified neither of professional women nor of any assaults, real or imagined, upon their dominion. In short, I am pleased that crime novels today have dared to confront both the dragon of gender stereotypes and the monsters of institutionalised injustice, whether of government, education or business. I rejoice to observe that the woman detective of today, like her brothers, is afraid neither of risk nor danger nor adventure, nor the power of hardened opinions and received ideas.

Women detectives take their chances, fight for justice without reward, because they improvidently believe in it, and know, even as their spirit and muscles hurt, that a life without struggle and growth is not life, but paralysis. And, in so acting, I believe that they encourage their readers to go and do likewise. That is, to enact their passion for justice, and to welcome situations they do not already know how to define.

KATHLEEN DAYUS

was born in Hockley, Birmingham, in 1903. Her childhood was spent in the slums of the city, in a district of small engineering works and metalworking foundries known as 'The Jewellery Quarter'. She left school at the age of fourteen to work at various jobs, including enamelling, before getting married in 1921. Left a widow with four young children when she was only twenty-eight, she experienced humiliating hardships and poverty. She now has twelve grandchildren and eight great-grandchildren. She still lives in Birmingham and was awarded an Honorary Master of Arts Degree by Birmingham University in 1992. Her first book of autobiography, *Her People* (1982), was followed by *Where There's Life*, *All My Days* and *Best of Times*. *The People of Lavender Court* is published in 1993.

HOW IT ALL HAPPENED
by KATHLEEN DAYUS

After I lost my second husband, I was lonely. My daughter Jean and her family were always asking me to stay with them, but I couldn't make my mind up as I liked to stay in my own home. Then, one Christmas I decided to visit for a few days. Little did I realise that this was to be the turning point of my life.

As I watched my young granddaughter Christina opening all her lovely presents, I began to think of those sad years long ago when I was about the same age.

'You are a lucky girl, Christina, to have a mum and dad to buy you such beautiful presents,' I said.

'What did you have then, Nan? When you was a young girl?' she asked.

'I only had an orange, an apple and a few monkey nuts in my stocking, sometimes a bright new penny. Once I never had nothing. It was a punishment for not darning the hole in my woollen stocking. It's a long story, Christina,' I added. 'But one day I may write a book about my life and my generation and when you're older I'll let you read it.'

'I'd love that, Nan,' she replied.

When I returned to my lonely house, I made myself a cup of cocoa, undressed and got into bed, but I was still thinking of writing about my life. I sat up in bed, pulled out some paper from the bedside drawer and began to write. Each night, for many months, when I couldn't sleep, I'd sit up in bed and write more and more about my working-class childhood, of the hopes and fears of growing up in ignorance, in the industrial slums of Edwardian Birmingham, the constant struggle with poverty, long hours of working life, constant ill-health and regular visits to the pawnshops.

My early widowhood at the age of twenty-eight forced me to relinquish my young children to Dr Barnardo's Homes. We were sleeping six in a bed in my mother's back-to-back bug-infested attic in the Hockley slums, known as the Jewellery Quarter, where I was born in 1903. I shall never forget the humiliation when I asked for help for me and my four young children during the Depression years when I became a widow.

Parish relief in those days was visits from the parish officers who came to see if you had anything to pawn or sell before giving you a meal ticket. I remember I sold firewood from door to door to eke out the money. I didn't tell them, so I was threatened with prosecution.

As soon as I finished writing my memoirs I pushed them in the bedside drawer and thought to myself: When I die my family can read them.

But several years later Christina asked me if I had written about my life. She was now sixteen and old enough to understand. I was pleased to think she took an interest so I gave it to her to read.

I was very much surprised when I heard that she had taken it to school for her teacher to read. The next wonderful surprise was that John Rudd came to see me and asked if I would like the manuscript published.

A few weeks later, Lennie Goodings and Ursula Owen from Virago Press came to visit and said they would be very pleased to publish my story.

My first book, *Her People*, was published in 1982, followed by *Where There's Life* and *All My Days*, to make a trilogy, and *Best of Times*. My first book brought me lots of happiness, meeting personalities, and being invited to booksellers where, one morning, I signed over three hundred books.

My next big thrill was winning the J.R. Ackerley Award and then Central Television came to do a documentary from my books. Imagine the excitement had when my daughter Jean and I took part, rehearsing the programme and meeting Lila Kaye, the film actress who took the part of my mother in the film, which was called *The Baker's Dozen*.

Another wonderful surprise was a letter from the BBC, asking me to appear on the Terry Wogan Show. I was fetched from Birmingham in a Daimler which drove me, my daughter Jean and her husband to the BBC in London. I can still recall the neighbours' curtains twitching as the Daimler drove us away.

I was a bit nervous at first, but Terry made me feel relaxed as he took my hand and led me into the beauty parlour, where the girls put on my 'war paint'. I couldn't believe it was me as I looked into the mirror, instead of looking my age – over eighty – I looked about fifty. When I got home after the show, I felt it was a pity I had to wash it all off. I was thrilled with the reception and the applause from the audience as Terry and I got chatting like old friends. Three days later I had another letter to say the audience wanted me back again for more chats. I was the only person to be on Terry's show twice in one week. The curtains twitched again as the Daimler drove up the second time, and my wonderful grandchildren had laid down a piece of red carpet on the path for me to walk along. I'm still living in hopes of meeting him again.

A few days ago I received a letter from Sir Michael

Thompson of Birmingham University to say I had been invited to accept the honorary degree of Master of Arts. I couldn't believe my eyes when I read about it. I had to read it again and again and now I'm to be measured for my cap and robe. I was so excited I rang my family and all my friends with this wonderful news.

Now, my family and I are going to celebrate at a restaurant in St Paul's Square facing the church where, as a young girl with other ragged barefoot children like myself, I took babies from our yard and sat them in my little 'go-cart' with a bottle of cold tea, and tied the cart to a tombstone while we played hide-and-seek. This is the same churchyard which we kids named 'Titty Bottle Park'.

Although it has had a face-lift with no more back-to-back slums surrounding it, it is still *my* Titty Bottle Park.

ANTONIA WHITE

(1899–1980) was born in London and educated at the Convent of the Sacred Heart in Roehampton, St Paul's and RADA. She worked as a copywriter and journalist until the Second World War when she was employed first by the BBC and then by the Foreign Office Political Intelligence Department. In the latter half of her life she became an acclaimed translator from the French.

Her first novel, *Frost in May*, which was later to launch the Virago Modern Classics series in 1978, was published in 1933, followed by *The Lost Traveller* (1950), *The Sugar House* (1952) and *Beyond the Glass* (1954). This quartet of novels became a major BBC TV serial in 1982. Antonia White's other work includes *Strangers* (1954), *The Hound and the Falcon* (1965), an account of her reconversion to Catholicism, and *Minka and Curdy* (1957), an enchanting story about her two cats. All these works are published by Virago.

Antonia White had two daughters, Susan Chitty and Lyndall Passerini Hopkinson, both of whom published books about their mother after her death. Susan Chitty has also edited her mother's early autobiography, *As Once in May* (Virago 1991), and Antonia White's *Diaries* recently published by Virago: Volume 1 1926–1958 and Volume II 1958–1979.

THE OLD DEMON, FEAR

by LYNDALL P. HOPKINSON

Antonia White is best known for *Frost in May*, her first novel written in the early 1930s. Of all her works published by Virago it is the one that has had most reprints since Carmen Callil 'rediscovered' it in 1978. But Antonia began to turn against her first novel when reviewers of subsequent books often compared them unfavourably to it; and twenty years after its original publication she complained, '*Frost in May* hangs round my neck like a withered wreath'. Also she did not consider it her best novel (she preferred *The Sugar House*), nor her best piece of writing, although it had brought her the recognition she thought she so desired when younger. She said in one of her diaries:

> The pleasure of feeling one has done good work is honestly greater than recognition. I am more glad to be praised for 'House of Clouds' because it seems to me better work [than 'Frost'] . . . done with no thought of anything but releasing a violent impulse to record something. Immediate stimulus of H[ouse] of C[louds] desire to display myself to Tom with whom I began to fall in love at that time.

The 'Tom' she mentions is Tom Hopkinson, whom she

met at the end of 1929 and would marry a year later; and 'The House of Clouds'* was a short story describing the nine months she had spent in Bedlam at the age of twenty-three, seven years before meeting him. The only clinical explanation for her sudden madness put forward at the time was that it might be 'the result of prolonged mental stress', for she had just ended her brief first marriage to a feckless and impotent alcoholic and a distressing nullity suit had followed.

Although Antonia noted there had been 'no pain whatever' in writing 'The House of Clouds' – 'in fact it took the "haunting" away' – that mysterious bout of madness had added the fear of insanity to her already long list of fears: fear of failure, fear of damnation, fear of disapproval and rejection, fear of loss, fear of the abyss, etc. And when, not long after having written about her madness, she was threatened with losing her mind again, and, in an attempt to save her sanity, agreed to undergo a full Freudian psychoanalysis, her 'old demon Fear' became a major theme in her diaries, though fear she greatly despised. 'It is far better to be sans peur than sans reproche. Fear is the real poison of the whole human race', she stated in 1937, while owning up to every kind of fear.

> Whatever I do I am in terror of losing something . . .
> It makes me equally afraid of religion and atheism, success and failure, love and celibacy . . . I wish to heaven I knew who I was – my old eternal cry . . . Until I can get rid of this paralysing fear, I can never have any happiness or be any use.

And yet such was her dilemma that she was afraid of losing fear lest, if that burden were lifted, she might become 'something really dangerous'. So terrified was she of what nature might have intended her to be as, through psychoanalysis, she became agonisingly aware of a 'violent drive' in her ('I need something to put it into or it turns against me'), and an incapacity to live by love ('love I have not'), that she asked herself whether perhaps she had to be ruled by fear in order not to be a 'menace' to others. 'Was I born to be hated?' she cried out in her despair.

Antonia claimed the fear of insanity was as abhorrent as the state of insanity. At the age of thirty-seven, during the Freudian analysis that would last four years, she wrote:

> In a way I fear sanity as much as insanity. I dread the *condition* of insanity, the responsibility of sanity. Sanity is a bogy: I confuse it with mediocrity, dullness, total lack of fire and imagination.

The bad mental state which had persuaded Antonia she needed analysis crept up on her as she attempted to write her second novel, which was to be about her father. It was heralded by headaches and nightmares and, after an attack of tonsillitis, by a profound depression. She was married to Tom at the time, and her symptoms are recorded more in his diaries than in hers, for she could not always describe her darkest moments while struggling through them. Antonia's state worsened when, while on holiday with Tom in Brittany, she discovered he had been having an affair with the wife of a friend. She now became suicidal and several times had to be forcefully restrained by him from throwing herself off the balcony of their fourth-floor flat. Later, while attempting to record the appalling mental state she had been in during and after that holiday, she said it had been worse in a way than the asylum because it all went on in actual life and ordinary surroundings:

I do not think I have ever suffered so sharply and persistently before. It was a complete disintegration, physical, mental, nervous and emotional.

Soon after starting to be analysed, she left Tom and her two children and went to live alone in a room in Chelsea for a while. During that period her notebooks read like a chronicle of despair, for it was also a time in her life when she was out of the Church and could not believe in God. There were days when analysis was so painful, 'like the reiterated drilling on an exposed nerve', that she felt like surrendering to madness. During one of those times she wrote:

It might be the will of God (do I speak literally or symbolically when I use those words?) that I should go mad again and again and perhaps, in the end, irretrievably. My value, my place in the scheme, if there is a scheme, might be just that. Have I a right to short-circuit it? . . . If I prayed to-day, and, as yet, I do not dare to, I would say 'Let me now not be afraid of going into myself or going out of myself. Let me be content to be anonymous, despised, intermittent . . . And let me not . . . be concerned in any way what happens to me, whether madness or sanity, fulfilment or frustration, provided only Thou wilt show me my right place, however humble, and keep me in it.'

With the help of analysis Antonia came through this mental breakdown, and soon afterwards returned to the Church. But she would continue to be daunted and haunted by the spectre of madness, and often in her dreams she was back in the asylum. And she suffered further black depressions. In her fifties, during one of them, she wrote to me 'I am not allowed to kill myself.

If I were not a Catholic I would.' And at the age of sixty-six she was treated for a year by a National Health psychiatrist who, she felt, helped her to avert a third mental breakdown.

To survive to the age of eighty-one with so piercing a sword of Damocles hanging over one's head takes courage. Antonia White deserves recognition for her bravery as much as for her writing.

PUBLISHER'S NOTE
* 'The House of Clouds', the story in which Antonia White gives a fictionalised account of her madness, and which is the particular focus of this essay, is from the collection of her stories, *Strangers*, published by Virago in 1981. It is also included in *Infinite Riches*, the anthology of stories from the Virago Modern Classics series, published to coincide with Virago's twentieth birthday.

JANETTE TURNER HOSPITAL

was born in 1942 in Australia, where she now spends half of each year, dividing the remainder between Canada and the United States. In 1982 *The Ivory Swing* won the Canadian Seal First Novel Award; it was followed, a year later, by *The Tiger in the Tiger Pit*. *Borderline* (1985) and *Charades* (1988) were each shortlisted for the Australian National Book Award; the latter was also shortlisted for the Miles Franklin Award. *The Last Magician* was published in 1992 to international acclaim and hailed by the *New York Times Book Review* as one of the most notable books of the year.

Janette Turner Hospital's short stories have been anthologised and published widely in magazines. Her first collection, *Dislocations* (1986), received the Fellowship of Australian Writers' Fiction Award; *Isobars* followed in 1990. She also reviews for the *New York Times*, the *Los Angeles Times* and the *TLS*. Janette Turner Hospital is Adjunct Professor of English at La Trobe University in Melbourne, and has also taught at Boston University. She is married with grown-up children.

Virago publishes all of the above works, with the exception of *The Ivory Swing* and *Dislocations*, which are forthcoming.

THE PERIPHERAL EYE
by JANETTE TURNER HOSPITAL

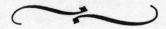

There's a story about Hannah Arendt that I love. I can't remember where I read it, and I can't find it again, so my version is suspect – but then all retellings are suspect. You cannot step into the same story twice, though the narrative eddies may lead you very pleasantly astray. I may have changed Hannah Arendt's intended destination (though I don't think I have); I may have embroidered things; but this is the way I recall the tale. *Caveat lector.*

Hannah Arendt was on her way to Columbia University where she was to deliver a well-publicised endowed lecture, but *en route* she became so vibrantly engaged in discussion with her taxi driver that she completely forgot the waiting dignitaries and the packed academic theatre. I sometimes picture her driver as a feisty Moshele, contentious, passionate, a Holocaust survivor, or a relative of others who perished, a man who read his newspapers and could tell her for a fact that there was nothing banal about evil, who could show her a street or two, a tenement or two, a nightmare or twenty ... But maybe he knew nothing about her at all, maybe he simply threw out a random question, and her mind, which was always on high voltage, seized on it and began to answer it from ten different angles. All I know is that they both

38

forgot where they were supposed to be heading, and they stopped for coffee somewhere, and went on talking and arguing while the Columbia organisers grew frantic and called the police and the hospitals and eventually, hours later, located her at her own apartment.

Oh dear, she probably said.

I love this story for sheepish reasons: it's the kind of thing I've been known to do myself. Taxi drivers, waiters, street kids, strangers in airports: they all seduce me. They are full of such astonishing stories, and their points of view are so unpredictable, so deliciously off-kilter, so not-the-same-as-mine. They render the familiar strange. I have interrupted taxi rides (though not when en route to major engagements; not yet, anyway); and I've gone off for drinks with waiters and/or waitresses after the restaurant meal. In foreign countries and unfamiliar cities I have wandered away with chance-met strangers on invitations that in retrospect have seemed a bit lunatic, and yet have led to unusual friendships and unorthodox points of view.

I have often felt embarrassed about this addiction to tangents. I have been furtive, practising digression in secret, always trying to placate those internalised judgements from childhood, school, university: *daydreamer . . . woolgatherer . . . hopeless . . . six directions at once . . . reckless . . .* what on earth were you *thinking* of?

Ah, what was Hannah Arendt *thinking* of?

How does the renegade thinker – the thinker as artist, creator, paradigm-shifter – think?

In circles, on parallel lines, on multiple tracks, via tangents.

Such messy thinkers are heretics. They don't think legitimately, (at least, not before they are declared innovative, original, *etcetera*). Until then, their thoughts are fuzzy, labyrinthine, muddled, wrong. So we're told. So I was taught. So I believed. I made countless resolutions to *pay attention*, to remain focused on the main event, to think in one prescribed and rigorous groove at a time.

To find Hannah Arendt as sudden kin, then, was heartening indeed – though I was hardly surprised that an unknown Manhattan taxi driver could sweep her off her intellectual feet, as it were, and out of the reach of an eminent but entirely predictable congregation of Columbia dons. Surely any lively mind knows this much: that the off-kilter observation, the 'uninformed' opinion, the muddled thought, the absolutely improper and inappropriate question can be galvanic. It is in those moments when the sensibilities are affronted, when the mind jumps tracks, that epiphanies come. Enlightenment lurks in the peripheral eye.

Tell all the Truth, wrote Emily Dickinson, *but tell it slant – Success in Circuit lies . . .*

Indeed. But it is much harder than we realise to see and to hear, let alone to retell, on the slant. Consider: while it is difficult to imagine trees more different in shape, in massiness, in colour, in bark, in leaf, than the English oak and the Australian eucalypt, it was decades before those officers and convicts of the First Fleet who were artistically inclined were able to draw trees around Sydney Cove that did not look like English oaks.[1] We think we see things as they are, but we don't. We see by formula, we tell by recipe. We slot things into what we already know in order to apprehend them at all. We have to be caught off guard, put at risk, shocked, in order to be jolted out of the limiting boundaries of our formulaic perception of the world.

'But why,' I once sighed to a friend in South India, 'why am I confined for hours and hours with the female relatives in the Hindu houses and then none of them will *talk* to me? I've tried and tried . . . I know my Malayalam is pretty hopeless, but even the ones who know English . . . I ask a question, and they answer·in a word, and that's it. They won't *talk* to me. I'm bored out of my mind, I'm going crazy.'

My friend pondered the question for a long time. He was South Indian, but from the Syrian Christian community with its western ties, and he had a married daughter in the States, though he himself had never been outside India. At last, he asked, puzzled: 'But why do you wish to talk to them, when you are not related?'

It was one of those moments of revelation. When you learn that you cannot even frame an intelligible question about a culture, you suddenly learn a great deal – much of it about your own conceptual limitations.

Incongruities, violations of our comfortable cognitive codes, cause disorientation, even pain, and certainly reactive anger – in life, in art, in science. Thomas Kuhn has noted that the first theorists of a new science (quantum physics, chaos theory, fractal geometry, whatever) are simply not perceived as following legitimate lines of enquiry. Their papers are not accepted at conferences, their articles are refused publication.[2]

The same can happen to novelists, though we have always, I think, been given a little more headroom. Well, not always. Consider the *Athenaeum*'s verdict on *Moby Dick* and its mad-eyed peripheral view: '. . . so much trash belonging to the worst school of Bedlam literature . . . [Mr Melville] seems not so much unable to learn as disdainful of learning the craft of an artist.'[3]

But the crafty artist insists on the renegade eye and ships out on tangents.

And so: once upon a time, when I was having a solitary lunch in the restaurant of the Sydney Opera House, I fell into lengthy conversation with my Chinese-Australian waiter who knew roads I had never travelled and who happened at the time to be reading, so he said, Marguerite Duras's *The Lover* which he wanted to discuss . . .

Somewhere else, on a different day, four men held a knife to my throat, and a pair of dilated eyes were six inches from mine. Night after night, they stayed there, six inches from mine. They lived under my pillow. They were wild, drug-hungry, malevolent and frightened; as frightened as mine, I think. What was it like to look out of such febrile eyes? What was it like to live the kind of life that led you to hold a knife at a woman's throat? I wanted to know, I had to know. I followed the eyes through nightmares and loops and tangents.

In a grimy coffee shop in Sydney, a fifteen-year-old hooker brandished her coffee spoon with disgust. 'You see that?' She pointed to the pin-hole in the spoon's curved bowl. 'They do it to stop us ripping off their spoons. We need them to heat the stuff, to juice up.' She needed other things too: seven men a day, seven days a week, to support her habit. She worked above a restaurant, the post-prandial treat.

Her friend, a university student, was in the flesh game just for the degree: 'I'll tell you something. After the first time, it's easy. And once you've done it for money, you have to think very hard before you'll do it again for free. Or just for the heck of it.'

Just for the heck of it, the Chinese-Australian waiter sent a postcard, a composed photograph that he had taken and developed himself, a bizarre and striking thing, his own hands a multi-fingered blur in front of the lens. 'Still Life with Fast Hand' he called it – and something bounced off his renegade eye and sent my imagination into ferment. He had given me the shape of an idea, then he fell away from that idea like a husk, and Charlie Chang presented himself fully formed, *pouf*, a bit of a magician from the start.

From these random seeds, and others, *The Last Magician* sprouted, and grew slant.

NOTES

1. Robert Hughes, *The Fatal Shore*, New York, Knopf, 1987, p.3.
2. James Gleick, *Chaos*, New York, Viking, 1987, p.35.
3. Bill Henderson (ed.), *Rotten Reviews*, New York, Penguin, 1986, p.61.

ALICE MILLER

lives in Switzerland, where for over twenty years she taught and practised psychoanalysis. Now she radically questions the validity of psychoanalytic theories and psychiatric methods and in 1988 resigned from the International Psychoanalytical Association. She has achieved worldwide recognition for her work on the causes and effects of child abuse, on violence towards children and its costs to society. Of her many books, which are translated into many languages, Virago publishes *The Drama of Being a Child* (1987), which first appeared in Britain in 1983 as *The Drama of the Gifted Child*, *For Your Own Good: The Roots of Violence in Child-rearing* (1987), *The Untouched Key: Tracing Childhood Trauma in Creativity and Destructiveness* (1990), *Banished Knowledge: Facing Childhood Injuries* (1990) and *Breaking Down the Wall of Silence: To Join the Waiting Child* (1991).

RECOVERY FROM
SELF-BETRAYAL

by ALICE MILLER
(Afterword to *More Revealed* by Ken Ragge)

Throughout time, people in distress have been seeking help from others: from sages, priests, gurus, psychologists and groups of different kinds. They have never known that, for the most part, out of all these people, none could lend real assistance because they too, like most other human beings, fear the only truth that can really help. That truth is about the origins of human suffering: the repressed tragic experiences of our childhood. The repression of injuries endured in childhood is the hidden cause of our later suffering.

For the child, this repression was necessary because otherwise he would have died from the overwhelming pain. However, adults need not die if they decide to become conscious. They can set themselves free from their symptoms and, at long last, be happy in themselves and in their lives as soon as they acknowledge the old wounds and let them heal. This becomes possible when we feel the strong emotions we had to repress in childhood in order to survive, when we take them seriously, clarify their meaning and learn that our pain and rage are justified. This happens when we condemn

46

the abuse without so-called moral objections and find our genuine, authentic needs. Anything else we may do, however well rooted in our culture and tradition, is betrayal and self-betrayal as long as it is based on the denial of truth and on the ignorance of real, provable knowledge.

What do we do if suddenly we hear unusual noises in our car? Or if we even suspect it is not running well? We take it to a skilled mechanic to find out what is wrong. We expect him to check the car and to find out why it is not running well before he proceeds to repair it. We would not entrust our car to a person uninterested in finding the cause of the problem or who would stubbornly dispute its importance. We would probably easily recognise that such a mechanic would make matters even worse.

But what we do for our car we are very often unable to do for ourselves. We often deliver up our souls without hesitation to exactly this kind of 'expert'. Why? Why are we able to take account of the skill of a person before we entrust him with our car but not with someone we decide to entrust with our soul? Is it because we learned from our parents early in our lives to ignore the existence of our soul: its laws, its plight, its despair and its needs? Is it because we learned to not care, to not feel the endured humiliations, to not know our rights, and to not ask questions? Is it because we are unaware of our own life history and don't want to know it for we are too afraid of feeling old pain? Or is it simply because we do not know how to feel this pain or that we can feel it safely? All these reasons, together, probably give the explanation. People abused and betrayed in childhood, and there are few who were not at the very least betrayed by 'poisonous pedagogy' (cf. Alice Miller, *For Your Own Good*), are not free to see through manipulation unless they lose their blindness in an effective therapy; they accept absurdities without resistance because that is what they are used to. Until recently, nobody actually knew how we could bring our forgotten (but stored up in our body and still very active) life history to light and, in this light, alleviate our pain. This concept has nothing to do with Freud and his followers. It is a new discovery, not yet taught in universities.

What would we do if we were hit by a reckless driver and left with a broken leg? We would have a doctor treat the injury as soon as possible so that it could heal properly. We would not go to a priest who would ask us to pray, or to an exorcist to cast out demons. Nor would we go to other people with broken bones who would treat our predicament as bad behaviour and advise us how to behave, who would lead us to believe that everything we have to do is to forget the pain and the broken bones and forgive the driver. At least where our bones are concerned, we would regard such demands as unreasonable and bizarre.

But again, not if it is a question of our soul. When our heart and our soul are broken we often go to ignorant and blind people who may even go so far as to ridicule our invisible but very real fracture. We go to people who cannot or do not want to understand because they are so terribly frightened of their own pain, pain over which they fear being misunderstood or ridiculed. They sometimes call themselves therapists but don't realise they are only trying to escape from their own painful history, to 'cure' themselves at our cost. They treat us according to the principles they themselves learned from their own childhood treatment: 'You must behave and remain lifeless, exactly as I was forced to do, you too must give up your feelings, your truth.' We also go to people who pretend to be the highest authority in 'recovery' today, but who use, uncritically, the poisonous pedagogy: 'We understand your anger with the driver, we even encourage you to feel it, but only for a while. Then you have to pull yourself together, let your feelings go, exercise "detachment" and "positive thinking" and, above all, you must forgive or else your bones will never heal.' 'Why not?' we should be able to ask. 'Isn't the recovery process dependent on the truth of the feelings and needs stored in our body? Don't our feelings and needs reveal important messages? Why do you want to take them away from us? Don't you realise how destructive your so-called "moral" chatter is?'

Even though this 'morality' is well rooted in our traditions and religions, killing one's feelings is contrary to Nature. Animals kill their young if they are sick and too weak to survive, but the healthy ones enjoy care and protection so they can live. Only the human child is condemned to an existence between life and death. It is no wonder so many people, looking for a means to escape this horror, end up addicted: to alcohol, to drugs, to overeating or to attending daily group meetings. But an addiction is not a safe refuge and, above all, it is no longer necessary. A different, healthy way to get rid of the horror has been found: to face it, to feel it, and to resolve its consequences. Even for those who have always tried to escape from their wounds because this seemed to be the one and only healthy way out, today, for the first time in our history, there is another option. We can make a choice. We can save our lives when we are prepared to search out our truth and when we refuse to be intimidated by the ridicule and ignorance of others. Now there is a method that enables us to access our life history, not with hypnosis, but by giving us complete leadership, autonomy and responsibility. This method has been very carefully developed by the Swiss therapist

J. Konrad Stettbacher and is set out in detail in his book, *Making Sense of Suffering* (Dutton, 1991). It has been tested by many people, myself included. Since the first German publication in 1990 we have learned that people can succeed, with the help of this description, to start their journey into their past, to discover their real biography and to alleviate even the most serious symptoms.

I think I owe this information to all those people who have written to me and who not only reject addiction as a way of dealing with problems and feared emotions but who also reject obedience as a way of adult life; to all those people who want to come in touch with their feelings and their truth, even if doing this work still frightens them; to people who are longing for a full life and do not know they have a right to it; to people who want to find their memories, memories locked up in frozen feelings, but who are unaware of the path leading to them. They are abstinent but suffer from depression or other forms of confusion and self-betrayal in spite of ten years or longer in various programmes. The way they use my information does not depend on me, but, for the most part, on their own life history. Once they start to explore this very history, they will escape from their plight and discover new options they never before could have imagined existed.

Dear Reader, when you read that I am recommending Stettbacher's method to heal, you should not follow blindly. You should check what I am saying on your own. You are free to discover if this therapy works for you or not. In any case, you do not have to believe in the 'higher power' to make it work. The 'higher power' will not do anything for you if you refuse to obey and refuse to remain blind. You have to do the work on your own with the help of Stettbacher's explanation. And you can do it because what you are going to find has always been within you. It has given you considerable anguish but only because it was denied, avoided and feared. Once you can face it, it will help you, it will guide you. You will recognise your fear as what it really is. Perhaps it is simply the fear of the child who is afraid of punishment if he acknowledges and speaks the truth. But you will not be punished now. Now, as an adult, you can insist on your right to feel your reality. You no longer need to cling to the empty word 'spirituality', a word that is meaningless because it is used for everything and says nothing that can't be said without using it. Your real, felt feelings will never kill you; they will help you find direction. Only the unfelt yet powerful emotions and needs, the feared and banished ones, can kill us.

Researchers are now beginning to grasp the truth that cancer can often be the last available, the ultimate, language of these repressed feelings. Therapists were surprised to see that once patients could feel, could express themselves, could take their unwanted emotions seriously and develop them into a direct and healthy language, full recovery was possible. (Cf. Linda Temoshock and Henry Dreher, *The Type C Connection*, Random House, 1992.)

To properly heal a broken bone you must consult a doctor. But the specific causes of your suffering can only be found by yourself. With the right instruction you can find them. When you are on the path towards your unique, unmistakable life history, you are mending your 'fractures'. Only one person can fully understand and heal them: you. The better you learn to take your feelings seriously and to understand them in depth with Stettbacher's technique, the quicker you will see through lies, humiliations and manipulations, and the more strongly you will be able to resist them.

What is addiction really? It is a sign, a signal, a

symptom of distress. It is a language that tells us about a plight that must not be understood. The drug business would not flourish if there were not so many people who, in refusing to acknowledge their wounds, are in a permanent state of self-betrayal. Thus, people work to get rid of symptoms instead of searching out the cause.

There are plenty of means to combat symptoms of distress: medication, sermons, numerous 'treatments', 'miracles', threats, cults, pedagogical indoctrination and even blackmail. They can all work for a while, but only because they reinforce the repression and reinforce the fear of resolving it. However, many people who become abstinent this way are driven into another addiction because the real reasons for becoming addicted must be kept hidden. A lot of money and fame comes from this business of repression because it satisfies the longings of so many grown-up children: to be loved as a good child (I am as blind as you want me to be. I am ready to forget all your cruelty, even at the cost of my life. Can you love me now?). In the long term, we have to pay a high price for this repression. The repressed story continues to try, again and again, to be heard at long last. Thus, your plight will look for other symptoms, another language, until it is taken seriously enough. [An addiction is an attempt by a person in despair, who is not allowed to be in despair, to get rid of his or her memory, to forget his or her plight. Of course, this 'solution' is no longer needed if the goal is exactly the opposite, if you want to remember, if you want to feel your plight and to understand its reasons, if you slowly become aware of why you were so afraid of acknowledging the reasons. This can happen once you decide to stop running away, to stop betraying yourself, to allow the truth to enter your consciousness. You decide to do so because you finally understand that everything else is useless and because you no longer want to watch your life go by before having even begun to live. You decide to stop betraying yourself because you understand that only you can give yourself the love and care you never received and that you can't do that as long as you deny the truth.

My recommendation of Stettbacher's therapy cannot be extended to any other I am familiar with. Unfortunately, therapists who are trained in this technique are still rare. If you feel that you need the help of somebody in becoming familiar with Stettbacher's method, or of someone simply as an 'enlightened witness' (Cf. Alice Miller, *Banished Knowledge*), you can look for a therapist who himself honestly tries to clear up his or her feelings and needs with the help of this method. If a person who calls himself a therapist tells you he doesn't need it, if he is not willing to thoroughly read *Making Sense of Suffering* and to work on it, but instead expresses general judgements; if he is obviously unable to discuss your questions concerning this therapy with you in detail, he will not be of any help to you. Sooner or later he will confuse you because of his own opposition and fears and he will impede the process of your liberation.

In any case, don't try to resolve the fears of your 'helpers'. If others refuse to do their work on their own, you cannot do it for them. No one can do it for anyone except for oneself. But you can refuse to pay the bill for their fears. You can refuse to let them use you to maintain their blindness. The more familiar you become with your biography, the better you will have learned to perceive your internal signals and take them seriously, and the easier you can judge whether people who call themselves therapists follow along with you and help you or whether they only serve to confuse you more. If you don't want to pay the bill for someone else's confusion, you must have the strength and the wisdom to give up a therapist as you would give up a mechanic who politely but blindly tried to fix your car while ignoring and wanting to ignore what was really wrong in the first place. He may be a nice person but as long as he can damage you, your life may be in danger. It is, then, your life that must have priority and nothing else.

KATE MILLETT

was born in St Paul, Minnesota, studied at the University of Minnesota and St Hilda's College, Oxford. Her first book, *Sexual Politics*, published in the USA in 1970 (Virago, 1977), was an immediate bestseller and established her at the forefront of feminist debate. Of her later books *The Loony Bin Trip* (1990; Virago 1991) is a startling and gripping account of her experience with American psychiatry. Kate Millett divides her time between her home in New York and her farm in Poughkeepsie in upper New York State.

PUBLISHER'S NOTE
Kate Millett offered us the following piece for the Keepsake, as 'she loves being a Virago author, and is very proud to be included'. It is the Introduction she wrote in 1990 for the new, paperback, edition of her novel *The Basement*, which first appeared in 1979.

MEDITATIONS ON A
HUMAN SACRIFICE

by KATE MILLETT

On 26 October 1965 the body of a sixteen-year-old girl named Sylvia Likens was found on a dirty mattress in a basement in Indianapolis, Indiana. Starved, mutilated, covered with cigarette burns, the victim had been imprisoned and tortured to death by a gang of teenagers led by a woman named Gertrude Baniszewski, in whose care Sylvia and her younger sister, Jenny Likens, had been left while their parents went off to work the state fairs in the Midwest.

Gertrude's band of tormentors included some of her own seven children, particularly her son John, twelve, and her daughter, Paula, seventeen, and two neighbour boys, Richard Hobbs and Coy Hubbard, both fifteen. On the abdomen of the young girl had been carved the words 'I am a prostitute and proud of it'. Sylvia had made one last attempt to summon help by pounding a coal shovel on the basement floor. The woman next door was just at the point of calling the police when the sound stopped.

Sylvia's death caught the others by surprise. Gertrude had John and Richard telephone the police and then lie to them that Sylvia had been set upon by a gang of boys after they 'got what they wanted' from her. With some foresight, Gertrude had forced Sylvia to write this tale out beforehand in a letter addressed to her parents. Jenny took one of the policemen aside: 'Get me out of here and I'll tell you everything.' The youngsters confessed; Gertrude never did.

The Basement 'happened' to me; there is no other word to describe the pain and shock of reading the story that first time, riddling over its hold upon me in the years that followed, haunted by it for fourteen years while building up the courage to 'do something' about it. When I wrote *Sexual Politics* I already knew about Sylvia Likens, already carried her inside me, but ten more years had to pass till I dared put down the words with which *The Basement* begins: Finally I can touch you with my voice, finally it's time, Sylvia Likens.

Life suggests an interest in certain stories; I was ambushed by this one early on and devoted my youth to it. My friend Fumio used to call it my myth of the Fall, both of us aware this was the chief story I would ever tell, the one temptation to fiction I might ever experience, because within it there was a compelling pattern, that single fable that explained all, the shadow at the back of the cave.

Of course it takes time to make something so over-whelming understood. It is foolish to be impatient. This is not didacticism or the logical highway of a doctoral thesis like *Sexual Politics*; this is closer to the mysteries, the tragic and symbolic, something finally inexplicable, something finally endured cathartically, that the heart changes – changes utterly. The need for liberation from sexual guilt and enslavement implicit in this historical event – for it is that too, not only a fictive puzzle or equation but an actual event more resonant and terrible than anything merely imagined – could transform us all, could burn away millennia of savagery. Savagery ongoing but exposed here, clarified, revealed so that it can no longer be lied about or ignored or dissembled or passed off as anything else, as something sexy or wicked or just twisted or senseless, a meaningless random event, something local or explicable through abnormal psychology or anthropology or subject to various interpretations.

This is the chill of an evil essentially collective, social, cultural, even political. It is the site of an old crime, old as the first stone, old as rape and beatings: it is not just murder, it is ritual killing; therefore the subtitle, *Meditations on a Human Sacrifice*. Maybe this is the real myth of the scapegoat; it was the daughter after all who was slaughtered, not the son. And for her, the actual victim, a patriarchal god provided no substitute. One looks into the brambles in vain and sees instead the lord of the flies.

It was a horrible death: like all deaths by torture the victim dies in the greatest physical anguish but broken-hearted as well, all that physical pain further compounded by psychological grief after having seen the hatred in one's tormentors' eyes – a hell of the mind as well as the body. To die this way. Alone and without comrades or cause, still a child. To know that much injustice.

But of course Sylvia's fate was extreme: in the early days of women's liberation we did not like to dwell on the violence against women which we began to see everywhere about us as the issues of rape and battered wives emerged almost in spite of our sporting and reasonable approach. Fair-minded arguments, we felt at first, would suffice to bring about equality; it was not necessary to dwell on atrocities. But once we began to acknowledge the cruelty and brutality which were the real foundation of patriarchy, what really kept it in power, we also had to acknowledge that the overwhelming, even puzzling, seemingly gratuitous violence practised towards us was fundamental. Now I began to analyse and to understand the power Sylvia's story had over me, for at first I had been helpless before it: feverish, afraid, annihilated, 'warned' in a curious sense – feeling, but not yet comprehending – victimised as the victim.

Gradually through the decade of the seventies I grew strong enough to absorb the meaning which this young girl's death had for me and the entire ritual of Sylvia's immolation took on a symbolic character, a metaphoric power. Of course we are broken in youth; of course we are shamed and then enslaved through shame: of course it is sexual shame. And here were people so naive they enacted the beliefs of the larger society, enacted them literally and, by going so 'overboard', exposed the brutality of its basic set of assumptions.

The atrocities we have learned to face under the rubric of 'child abuse' were still scarcely understood in 1980 and easily confused with the taboo, the obscene, and the sensational. *The Basement* shocked and sickened. Even feminists, or perhaps feminists in particular, were so upset by Sylvia's suffering and Gertrude's perfidy – this cruelty in one of us – that the book frightened and alienated what might have been its first natural readership. Reviews were respectful but the fact remained that to read the book at the time of its first appearance was an intensely painful experience. Yet no one who read it forgot. The dramatic possibilities inherent in the text appealed to several venturesome theatre directors: Godard even thought of filming it. But it was too early. The hardcover first edition was remaindered. The book I had waited all those years to be good enough to write had misfired; it was the greatest disappointment in my life as a writer.

So much for my own pique: more to the point, I had to realise that since no one had heard me, no one had rescued Sylvia either. I had to acknowledge my enormous expectations: of course, I had almost always realised that I could not save the life of this dead girl, but I had once imagined I could prevent other deaths – those of the next victims. It was for this reason I'd spent those years preparing myself to come forward as Sylvia's champion, to intervene and explain the cruel stupidity of her death, even the contemptible social logic in the general persecution of young womanhood. All to prevent its recurrence.

At first it merely seemed that we had left out part of the feminist argument, a crucial point about sexual shame. The minute this oversight was rectified and the analysis complete, the oppression of our youngest and most vulnerable sisters, even of our own earlier selves, would be clarified and relieved. In my own private code I thought of this book as *Sexual Politics II*. I had meant *The Basement* to do things, to save lives. If not physically, then psychologically. Because it's at Sylvia's age that every woman's neck is broken; and those who do it are rarely dumb or obvious enough to get caught with the evidence.

Yet all along there was Gertrude. Gertrude was a paradox, a contradiction, a mistake in the column of figures; how can you blame patriarchal institutions when they are enforced by a woman? Just the point: no system of oppression operates without collaborators. Gertrude is a kapo, an agent. Victim herself originally, but in time a true believer in her own unworthiness and in betraying her kind, no less a victimizer. Back then this was still bad news around the feminist campfire; I remember my friend Ti-Grace's ironic warning over the phone that there would be hell to pay on the ideological front. But we always knew this, I protested, it even figures. Sure, she chuckled, it's just a point some don't feel ready to concede publicly. If women in the movement could not bear to bring themselves to read of Sylvia's suffering, they could bear still less to face Gertrude's complicity.

It was the same for me in the beginning, that's why it took me so long to start the book, arrive at a point of view, a tone, a path through the hell that waited just outside the door all those years Sylvia needed me to rescue and defend her, valorize and explicate her agony. All those years I failed to do so.

I remember finally holding the transcript at last, reading it so eagerly I didn't bother to sit down, standing by my little oak table in the Supreme Court in Indianapolis, and being so sickened by certain details that I was dizzy and afraid of falling, afraid of the photographs, afraid of going on. This much horror was what I'd been running away from all along; the mind would not be able to bear it. One would go mad, I had thought at the beginning.

In fact it seems I had to be at least declared mad before I could risk getting this far. My first reaction to Sylvia Likens's story was to sculpt it over and over again in exhibition after exhibition: sculptures that were large wooden cages, cages with things and people in them, oblique retellings, indirect versions of this central event dispersed into general references to politics and society within a fairly surreal context, but all based upon this original myth. For over ten years I continued obsessively to put forth this experience in visual terms but I dared not approach it in words. Not until I had fallen through the rabbit hole and tumbled down into the pit: not till the first loony-bin trip.

After that, literature scared me a lot less. The old bogy of falling over the edge, 'losing' one's mind, was so tired and familiar and without terror by now, I could even hazard conjuring up Gertrude. That is, I could dare to realise I already knew all about her. So do we all; the problem is simply admitting it. And having myself undergone a 'disappearance' into the labyrinth, having survived capture and my own dark nights wondering if I would ever see freedom again, I could begin to spin words and imagine Sylvia's last days in that basement. Now that I knew fear: not as she knew it, but imagination could do the rest, bridge the gap, persuade. Mirror tricks of course, but you don't try them till you know something about mirrors and the nature of the truth being reflected.

Composing an introduction today, ten years after having written the book's conclusion, hoping that this time I will find those to vindicate her, I realise too that when I imagined Sylvia's death as transcendence of circumstances she could master no other way − escape having failed her in the fact of her fate − I deliberately imagined this death as victory because I refused to entertain the utter despair which jostled against it. Death is certain escape on some occasions, even a happy ending when none other is possible.

I also made her, this girl, a tomboy, an androgyne, a mind, a cutup, a rebel, one who drew fire, whom abuse could cow into capitulation as we are all cowed and all capitulate, humbled and betrayed and in the darkness lost, able only at the end to dare to live, to be the worm who turns, and when cornered finally, to stand and curse the godly, probably even God. Yet then with one great act of determination, so enormous it is the first moment of a new life − able to will one's own death. This is to beat the odds, to see slavery ahead and refuse it: this is to seize freedom even if one has to invent it. She would endure no more, she would wait no longer. A great tide had turned, even then; now it builds a wave.

GRACE NICHOLS

was born in Georgetown, Guyana, where she grew up and worked, among other things, as a reporter and freelance journalist. She came to Britain in 1977 and since then has written a number of children's books, including a collection of poems, *Come On In To My Tropical Garden* (1988), and edited an anthology of poems for children. Her first book of poems for adults, *i is a long-memoried woman*, was winner of the 1983 Commonwealth Poetry Prize. *The Fat Black Woman's Poems* (1984), *Lazy Thoughts of a Lazy Woman* (1989) and her novel, *Whole of a Morning Sky* (1986), are published by Virago. She is currently working on a new cycle of poems for which she has been awarded an Arts Council bursary. She lives in Britain.

PSYCHIC CONNECTIONS
by GRACE NICHOLS

My voice as a writer has its source very much in the Caribbean region, which means that psychically you're at once connected to the Americas, Africa, Asia and Europe. I've always found this cross-fertilisation creatively exciting, the ability to move among and be influenced by the different cultural strands, in terms of language, food, religion.

In my first cycle of poems, *i is a long-memoried woman*, I dealt with my female historical past – the streams of memory of a slave woman, who for me embodies all the women who've gone through that humiliating and brutal experience, but who is a woman that emerges with a spiritual strength and the ability to appraise her situation:

> I have crossed an ocean
> I have lost my tongue
> from the root of the old one
> a new one has sprung
>
> (Epilogue: *i is a long-memoried woman*)

Although memory and the politics of oppression feature strongly in my work I also claim the right to be true to the other sides of my personality; to my sense of fun and my laid-back musings, as evident in the following poems from *Lazy Thoughts of a Lazy Woman*. (Most of the poems in this book were written during the early stages of my pregnancy a few years ago, which gave me a good excuse for putting my feet up and observing):

Dust

Dust has a right to settle
Milk the right to curdle
Cheese the right to turn green
Scum and fungi are rich words.

Grease

Grease steals in like a lover
over the body of my oven.
Grease kisses the knobs
of my stove.
Grease plays with the small
hands of my spoons.
Grease caresses the skin
of my tablecloth,
Getting into my every crease.
Grease reassures me that life
is naturally sticky.

Grease is obviously having an affair with me.

With Apologies to Hamlet

To pee or not to pee
That is the question.

Whether it's sensibler in the mind
To suffer for sake of verse
The discomforting slings
Of a full and pressing bladder

Or to break poetic thought for loo
As a course of matter
And by a-peeing end it.

Wherever I Hang

I leave me people, me land, me home
For reasons, I not too sure
I forsake de sun
And de humming-bird splendour
Had big rats in de floorboard
So I pick up me new-world-self
And come, to this place call England
At first I feeling like I in dream –
De misty greyness
I touching de walls to see if they real
They solid to de seam
And de people pouring from de underground
   system
Like beans
And when I look up to de sky
I see Lord Nelson high – too high to lie

And is so I sending home photos of myself
Among de pigeons and de snow
And is so I warding off de cold
And is so, little by little
I begin to change my calypso ways
Never visiting nobody
Before giving them clear warning
And waiting me turn in queue
Now, after all this time
I get accustom to de English life
But I still miss back-home side
To tell you de truth
I don't know really where I belong

Yes, divided to de ocean
Divided to de bone

Wherever I hang me knickers – that's my home.

Of course living in England for the last fifteen years
how can I help being influenced by such phenomena as
tea-drinking, the weather, that breathless rush to catch
trains and the slimming industry:

The Fat Black Woman Goes Shopping

Shopping in London winter
is a real drag for the fat black woman
going from store to store
in search of accommodating clothes
and de weather so cold

Look at the frozen thin mannequins
fixing her with grin
and de pretty face salesgirls
exchanging slimming glances
thinking she don't notice

Lord is aggravating

Nothing soft and bright and billowing
to flow like breezy sunlight
when she walking

The fat black woman curses in Swahili/Yoruba
and nation language under her breathing
all this journeying and journeying

The fat black woman could only conclude
that when it comes to fashin
the choice is lean

Nothing much beyond size 14

MICHÈLE ROBERTS

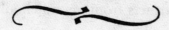

born in 1949, is half-English, half-French, and now lives in London. She has published two collections of her own poetry, and co-authored four volumes of short stories. An acclaimed novelist (*A Piece of the Night*, *The Visitation*, *The Wild Girl*, *The Book of Mrs Noah*, *In the Red Kitchen*), she was shortlisted for the 1992 Booker Prize for her sixth novel, *Daughters of the House*, published by Virago. She has been Visiting Fellow of Creative Writing at the University of East Anglia and a collection of her short stories, *During Mother's Absence*, will be published by Virago in 1993.

Daughters of the House received the W. H. Smith Literary Award for 1992.

Writing DAUGHTERS OF THE HOUSE

extracts from my notebooks

by MICHÈLE ROBERTS

August 1989 The new novel will examine: the problem of dialogue/the problem I have with dialogue; and so the problem of character, my unbelief in real objective characters and so my problem with people in texts speaking to each other. Also it could examine a new way of letting the text embody the practice of making – rather than just letting the text embody itself as diary or gospel or autobiography or letters or whatever, let the prose itself demonstrate that it's *written*: this will free the narrative and free the voices I want to use. Let the narrative twist and turn like a glass focusing and refocusing from different perspectives, so that we see the texture, opacity and colour of the glass, the prose itself.

Also to describe a mother-daughter relationship that is really close and loving. Imagine it.

Perhaps the child of the English-French couple will speak in tongues? As well as having visions. She can only tell the reader/her parents about it; we can't share the experience. Though I think the mother longs to do so, and is devastated that she can't. Bits from the daughter's point of view? The mother writing a memoir of her daughter? Who dies young, or what? The daughter writing her spiritual autobiography? When I was young how ardently I longed to know God by personal revelation, to see visions like the saints did. Later I transferred this longing to the writing of poetry – and indeed did experience bliss when a poem came, though I know now that this is a feeling rooted in the body, the bliss of giving all joyfully that the baby feels, when shitting for example! When I was younger and split the spiritual so severely from the physical I couldn't tolerate knowing that.

The novel will concern things which are not there to be seen, things which cannot be spoken. God. Hatred. The breast!

Connected to this is my wish to write about envy.

But one of the reasons I'm stuck writing the novel is perhaps that I've begun at the beginning? And would feel easier just writing odd bits as they pop up? As I did long ago with *A Piece of the Night* – a process which terrified me, it felt so crazy.

The novel has begun to suggest itself to me – its form and structure. But I can't write it. I've written four pages of rubbish. I can't write. I can't write poetry either.

April 1990 The vision – seen by a little girl no one trusts – of a black lady with red lips and loose black hair, a black sexy madonna. The narrator goes out at night, picks men up, has sex – it's her perhaps the little girl has seen?

Dream: I was with a large group of people inside some sort of large building. I had a vision, in common with them, of the Virgin – it developed slowly, like a photograph, in red – I was very excited, being granted something I had wanted for so long. She was not particularly beautiful – she had a big nose, quite ugly.

(Next day) I went to see Amanda Faulkner's new works in her studio: there was that red madonna, exactly as in the dream.

NB: there should be a good quarrel going on between the women.

A biography that tells as much about its writer as about its subject?

Inner *and* outer worlds this time.

The narrator can speak as an 'I' and also refer to Leonie – we discover late on that 'I' is Leonie.

Went to the Royal Academy to look at the 20th Century Modern Masters exhibition. Sat and looked at the Matisse and felt I knew about the joy and bliss of the world, directly, in my body, just as I know about grief and sadness too. This was the day I finally started my new novel. This morning I sat and wrote about the red lady that the child sees. Half a page. A beginning. Only recently did I realise that the reason I could not start to write it was because Jackie is dying and it seemed obscene, also simply impossible, to write.

June 1990 Problems I want to tackle: using autobiographical material, how to do it; writing about the past; trying to keep 'myself' 'the author' out of the story, i.e. name this as a problem, make it part of the subject, exploit it; using an omniscient narrator, which I've always felt I shouldn't do, i.e. break this taboo, exploit it.

Feminine/feminist writing: from the margins, through a peephole, from a deliberately limited perspective; exploit all this.

Narrative: one sister talking about the other. Swap dialogues and quarrels. Two narratives that quarrel with each other.

An inventory of the things in the house? Doesn't have to be realistic after all. A story about each item? And all the stories might link up somehow in the end. Also the content of the items could fight against the form of the list.

NB: Charles's tale of the Parisians who try to go for

weekend walks across his land – he alters the electric fencing, uses it to bar their passage. He laughed in triumph. He talked about beating women: in the old days we did it with bouquets but now with our bare hands.

The cross-Channel boat is very important because it's Leonie's connection of England and France – her journey – as well as what separates them.

September 1990 I want to write about envy surfacing – huge strong envy – murderous fantasies! She'll want to steal from the other woman – or even kill her to get what she wants.

Make it an inventory of things not just in a particular house but in a person's mind. Images to do with the war. NB: that Gestapo shopping-list: metres of yellow material for stars, curtaining for vans, trains for deporting Jews, handcuffs and weapons.

Such gloom and despair today such depression such feelings of total failure. Not a word of the novel would come. Felt trapped powerless hopeless.

A certain grim pleasure in finding out for the first time in my life that I can write a novel and not smoke. Work work work sleep work work work. I'd like to fly off and be thoroughly irresponsible. I would like a holiday, that's what I'd like.

March 1991 The book must start with the spectre of Nazism rising from the grave. That's what makes Thérèse come back.

Intense pleasure. I must record it now in case a year from now I'm in the thick of another novel and can't believe I'll ever get clear. Intense pleasure because I'm at the end, I know what the ending is, having spent the last month thrashing around and not knowing and despairing and feeling the novel was about to fall into unmendable bits. It's a whole; made of bits; it fits together; and I've just discovered that.

Dream: I was in a convent. A nun and I were tending the body of a dead woman, caring for it as though preparing it for burial. The dead woman was X, the part of her that's bitter and frustrated, and it was me, the part of me that was like that or is like that. Dead and buried, but treated with respect and care not just thrown away. It wasn't spirituality or women's communality that I was letting go of; but bitterness, ashes; old griefs.

So at the end of the novel Leonie has her vision of Rose with two babies, then of Antoinette's body which she prepares for burial?

Thérèse with her back on fire. Running. A fin of fire. A wing of flame.

She rises. She rises. Up out of the grave she comes, that red girl, with her terrible truth.

August 1991 Staying in Carl and Julie's house in Escuillens. I love it, this life of meeting neighbours and having a chat, people popping in and out, hearing the vans arrive and running out to buy melons or bread. I sit at the typewriter, village life goes on in the street beyond the garden hedge, I work and chat. Last night I dreamed of Jackie. We were in our beds in our old room in the old house, and she came over to my bed and whispered in my ear: I've written you a letter in which I've put down all the secrets I've ever known.

LYNNE SEGAL

was born in Sydney, Australia. She received a doctorate in psychology from Sydney University, then came to London with her fourteen-month-old son. Since then she has taught psychology at what is now Middlesex University and has been involved in feminist and socialist politics; she is a member of the *Feminist Review* collective and participated in the launching of the national Socialist Society. Her works include *Is the Future Female?: Troubled Thoughts on Contemporary Feminism* (Virago, 1987), *Beyond the Fragments* with Sheila Rowbotham and Hilary Wainwright (1979), *Slow Motion: Changing Masculinities, Changing Men* (Virago, 1990) and *Sex Exposed: Sexuality and the Pornography Debate* with Mary McIntosh (Virago, 1992). She lives in London.

A CREATURE OF DECADES

by LYNNE SEGAL

I am a creature of decades. It was a familiar narrative, a lucky narrative, embedded in a very particular historical moment and milieu, that brought me to writing. I arrived in England from Australia in 1970, thoroughly lost and confused. A young single mother imbued with sixties radicalism, I rejected the only potential identities seemingly open to me, as 'academic', 'wife' or 'full-time mother', when, unplanned and unexpected, I was rescued from the isolation and fear this landed me in by women's liberation.

Throughout the 1970s, while teaching psychology at Middlesex Polytechnic, I was also immersed night and day in local feminist and libertarian socialist politics in north London – dashing from meeting to meeting, march to march, learning, talking, writing, invigorated by a passion and purpose intrinsic to those years. Some of all this went into my section of *Beyond the Fragments: Feminism & the Making of Socialism* (first published in 1979 by Islington Community Press, reprinted by Merlin Press), written with the support and inspiration of its main author, Sheila Rowbotham. Beyond the expectations we shared, it was, for a brief moment, a fortunate publication. Extremely popular in radical circles at the close of the seventies, it seemed to encapsulate the surviving hopes of the grassroots politics of that passing decade. Little though we realised then, however, as over a thousand optimists gathered in Leeds to discuss the implications of the book, it was the beginning of the end of it all.

Ironically, the decline of such activism in the 1980s gave me the time to write more. In 1984 Ursula Owen suggested I write some type of assessment of contemporary feminism and its future for Virago, and invited me to join the Advisory Board to suggest similar books which they might commission and publish. It was very much her support which led to my first book, *Is the Future Female?: Troubled Thoughts on Contemporary Feminism*. I needed a lot of encouragement in those days, and to feel (oh what a luxury!) that there would be some political response to what I was writing.

Is the Future Female? addressed things that were worrying me at the time in a growing feminist orthodoxy very much at odds with earlier socialist feminist activity and analysis, itself fast disappearing from public debate and official feminist history. I regretted the move towards a greater emphasis on fixed sexual *difference*, and the politics accompanying it. New feminist mythologies, I suggested, were replacing the more subtle analysis of complexity and ambiguity determining both similarities and differences in women and men's access to power, experiences and lives – found, for example, in writing like that of Sheila Rowbotham (a selection of which is available today in *Dreams and Dilemmas*, Virago). The diverse nature of women's struggles and problems could not be reduced simply to gender, nor could they be resolved by the assertion of *female* values. This book explored the types of feminist theorising and practices which might, I felt, point towards worlds closer to different women's more particular needs and desires. Many of the ideas I criticise in that book, which originate in the 'cultural feminist' perspectives of writers like Andrea Dworkin, Mary Daly, Susan Griffin and others from the USA, have become even more influential since then.

Again encouraged to keep on writing by Ursula Owen and Ruthie Petrie, my next book, *Slow Motion: Changing Masculinities, Changing Men*, was a sequel to *Is the Future Female?* It addressed the nature of 'masculinity', asking when and why men embark upon or resist change. Aiming to promote a more positive sexual politics for the 1990s, it challenged the conservative pessimism, now frequently endorsed by feminists (and accompanying more conservative times generally), which suggests that we have not seen, and should not expect to see, significant change in men's use and abuse of power and privilege. On this view, feminist policies to construct women's equality with men are doomed, indeed can render women even more vulnerable, because men don't change. Yet the historically changing nature of 'masculinity', its contemporary diversity and the complex and contradictory nature of sexual identity, both male and female, suggests otherwise. 'Masculinity', I argued here, exists not as any fixed attributes shared by all men, but rather in the various institutional and symbolic forms of power which men are more likely to have access to. Giving both positive and negative examples, I illustrated the possibilities and the problems determining whether, and how, men change, which men are most likely to change, and whether or not such change makes a difference to men's customary privileges and authority. Change in men is possible, I argue, but it is as much an ideological and social struggle as a personal struggle.

Now, at the beginning of the 1990s, I continue to write on similar themes connecting sexuality, personal life and politics. They reflect my own political formation in the sexual politics of the 1960s and the critique, extension and femininisation of those ideas in the passionate beginnings of women's liberation. I am always returning to the different ways in which sexuality and personal life become interwoven with both radical and conservative political moments and movements.

Very much along these lines, Mary McIntosh and I edited *Sex Exposed: Sexuality and the Pornography Debate*. This collection illustrated once again how thoroughly feminists have divided over the last decade on questions of sexuality and its representation, culminating in the currently embattled positions of the Campaign Against Pornography (CAP) and Feminists against Censorship (FAC). The collection tried to offer something new in the face of the entrenched polarity between those who see pornography as the key to women's oppression and liberal blindness to the need to engage with and reject sexist and racist representation and practices. My own contribution to this collection, and my ongoing writing, is a continuing exploration of heterosexuality – its history, discourses, pains and pleasures. Here I want to move beyond the negative theorising heterosexuality has received from feminists over the last decade, to capture instead the volatile fluidity of sexual experience, which potentially always transcends all the dreary dichotomies of gender, power and agency. Not so easy, but absorbing; quite necessary to survive these dark days of political apathy and depression.

ELAINE SHOWALTER

was born in 1941 in Cambridge, Massachusetts, and educated at Bryn Mawr College and the University of California. From 1967 to 1984 she taught English and Women's Studies at Rutgers University, and she now chairs the Department of English at Princeton University. Her first book, *A Literature of Their Own: From Charlotte Brontë to Doris Lessing*, was published by Virago in 1978. She edited *The New Feminist Criticism: Essays on Women, Literature and Theory* (Virago, 1986) and *These Modern Women: Autobiographies of Women in the 1920s*. She wrote *The Female Malady: Women, Madness and English Culture 1830–1980* (Virago, 1987) and an acclaimed study of gender and culture at the *fin de siècle*, *Sexual Anarchy* (Virago, 1992). Her collection of short stories by women writers of the same period, *Daughters of Decadence*, appears in 1993.

WRITING A LITERATURE
OF THEIR OWN
by ELAINE SHOWALTER

I n June 1970, the month that I gave birth to my
second child, I received my PhD from the University
of California at Davis, for a dissertation about the
ways that Victorian reviewers applied a double critical
standard to women's writing. When I set out to write
the thesis in 1965 there were few precedents for such a
scholarly enterprise, and the final product was cautious
and understated; but given the unfashionability of the
topic, the biases against hiring and promoting women
professors, and the absence of maternity leave or day
care, it was a miracle that I had persisted with it at all.

By the time I finished, however, the mood of the country had changed, and I had become an active member of
the women's liberation movement. As the issues in my life
and my work took on new meaning through feminism, I
began to envision a much bolder critical undertaking, and
to imagine a *feminist* literary criticism that would do for
the history of women's writing what Northrop Frye had
done for Canadian literature, or even what Perry Miller
and F. O. Matthiessen had done for American literature.
Hitherto, virtually all critical generalisations about 'wom-
en's literature' had been based on a tiny group of novelists

– Jane Austen, the Brontës, George Eliot, Virginia Woolf. I set myself the task of filling in the gaps, of reading as many novels by British women in the nineteenth and twentieth centuries as I could find, and then beginning to work out the ways in which they related to each other. If there *was* a female literary tradition, I was sure, it was not because women were biologically different to men, nor because they were inherently more interested in romance or homemaking. Women's writing had to do with literary conventions and the pressures of the marketplace, with professional self-image and critical reception.

With the help of a fellowship from Rutgers University, I spent the year 1972–3 in London, tracking down the books, manuscripts, letters and diaries of scores of British women writers. Most days I worked in the dusty hodge-podge of the Fawcett Library, then a fabulous but largely uncatalogued collection on women supported by the stalwart members of the British Suffragette Fellowship; or in the Reading Room of the British Museum. Frequently I went on the road to municipal public libraries around Britain in search of materials, and sometimes I was rewarded in some chilly, dimly lit room by being the first person to open a box of letters or to read a harrowing journal.

Being part of a great movement in history sustained me on the days when the trains were late and the boxes were empty, when I couldn't figure out how to put the story together, and words failed me. But what really kept me going were the women writers themselves. I kept finding passages in their letters about the future, about their own failures and limitations, and their hopes that all the struggles and sorrows of their lives would make a difference to the women who would come after. There was the novelist Geraldine Jewsbury, writing to her friend Jane Carlyle in the 1840s:

I do not think that either you or I are to be called failures. We are indications of a development of womanhood which is not yet recognised ... There are women to come after us, who will approach nearer the fullness of the measure of the stature of a woman's nature. I regard myself as a mere faint indication, a rudiment of the idea of certain higher qualities and responsibilities that lie in women, and all the eccentricities and mistakes and miseries and absurdities I have made are but the consequences of an imperfect formation, an immature growth.

There was the South African feminist writer Olive Schreiner, describing herself as part of a tragic generation of women in the 1890s who would have to sacrifice love for freedom so that future generations could have both. And of course there was Virginia Woolf in *A Room of One's Own*, saying to women that, 'if we have the habit of freedom and the courage to write exactly what we think,' if we work together, 'the dead poet who was Shakespeare's sister', the poet who 'lives in you and in me, and in many other women who ... are washing up the dishes and putting the children to bed', will be born again. 'As for her coming without that preparation, without that effort on our part, without that determination that when she is born again she shall find it possible to live and write poetry, that we cannot expect, for that would be impossible. But I maintain that she would come if we worked for her, and that so to work, even in poverty and obscurity, is worth while.'

Jewsbury, Schreiner, Woolf and others gave me the confidence to believe that it was all right if I myself were not, say, F.R. Leavis's sister – the great woman critic who would get everything right. It was enough to try to be worthy of the women I was writing about, to find the courage to write exactly what I thought, and to be willing to share my own mistakes and absurdities in the faith that those critics who came after would know more, and that they would find it easier to live and to write.

Thanks to Virago, *A Literature of Their Own* transcended its beginnings in an American university press to reach the wider reading audience in Britain for whom it had really been written, and in the last twenty years scores of those lost women writers of the past have come back from obscurity to be rediscovered in their green Virago dresses by a new generation. May the next twenty years bring Virago, and feminist criticism, continued health, productivity, and the habit of freedom!

GILLIAN SLOVO

was born in South Africa in 1952. Both her parents were courageous political activists, and the family was forced into exile in 1964. They settled in London where she still lives. Gillian Slovo has written three detective novels, as well as *Ties of Blood*, and *The Betrayal*, a political thriller set in South Africa and published by Virago. *Facade*, her most recent novel, will be published by Virago in 1994.

ANOTHER TRUTH

by GILLIAN SLOVO

S unday in November: an arts centre, a converted Baptist chapel, in southern England. I was on stage and, having finished my introductory talk, had begun to read a short passage from *The Betrayal*.

I didn't get far. Two paragraphs in I misread a word, putting 'detention' in 'detection's' place. My fellow speaker, who had spent the weekend incarcerated with me in a library teaching crime fiction, chortled. Which set me off: I, too, began to laugh.

The audience was politely waiting. I stopped, straightened my face and relaunched myself into my reading. But when my tongue tripped on the same, unfunny sentence, my laughter surged. I laughed so much that the audience joined in. I surpassed them. I laughed so much, my cheeks were wet.

'Now we know what it means to laugh until you cry,' commented my friend. I nodded agreement. But even in that embarrassing moment I knew that what was really happening was that I was laughing not until, but instead of, crying.

It had been a hard weekend. Workshops can be exhausting and this public event came at the end of a day of heavy concentration and little food. Yet what had set me off was not fatigue: it was a long wait in a strange house at the end of which I discovered that someone, a woman younger than me, a once lively, laughing woman whose photographs were everywhere in evidence, had recently killed herself there.

My laughter was, I suppose, a release from the horror of this act and also a different kind of release. Two days before I had handed in the final proofs of my latest book – *Facade*. *Facade* is another kind of thriller – a book about a successful, lively woman who is struggling with the beckoning shadow of a powerful mother who years ago had killed herself.

Some books come easy – *Facade* did not. It ends with a siren call and during moments of its writing, I feared that it had become my self-created siren call. The subject was dark, of course, but I always suspected that my difficulties did not stem from this fact alone. There was something inside of me that made the book both powerful and difficult and while I wrote it I kept wondering in which bit of my own unconscious did its inspiration lie.

Not a question, as I found out early in my fiction writing, that is ever easy to answer. My first books featured a detective investigating murder. In answer to the inevitable 'Why genre and why this one?' I had a number of replies. I liked detective fiction, I'd say, and strong narratives and tight rules which I could then try and break. All of which was true but which was also only a part of the truth. For what I, in hindsight, have realised is that I chose to write crime because of my background. The daughter of two South African political activists, I'd had a childhood full of tension, sudden disappearances, grown-ups who left the house and went into the garden when they wanted to talk. And so when I came to write crime these elements – the build-up of tension, the unexpected happenings, the unheard conversation waiting to be uncovered – were second nature to me.

Three books later, the rules felt suffocating. I moved away from their restraints. I went deeper, I think, into the next layer, into the fear perhaps behind my childhood's mysteries. The latest is *Facade*.

That day in November, I never did manage to finish my reading. My fellow speaker took over and, with the evening finished, we took a train back to London. I arrived home at 2 a.m., too wired to go to bed. So I opened my post. And saw there a section from a book somebody is writing about my mother's journalism. I picked out the chapter that dealt with my mother's time in prison. I sat, reading of it, of the book she had written about her detention and of how it had ended in her collapse and in her suicide attempt. I had of course always known of my mother's action, and yet now, after my crying laughter, I knew it differently.

That early morning the final piece of the puzzle had slipped into place. Or had it? That's what's so wonderful about writing fiction: what you don't know can be as important as what you do and always, somewhere, can lie another truth.

DEBORAH TANNEN

was born in Brooklyn, New York. She received her PhD in linguistics from the University of California, Berkeley, and has been awarded fellowships and grants from many organisations, including the Rockefeller Foundation, the National Endowment for the Humanities and the National Science Foundation. She has thirteen books and over seventy articles to her name, and became an internationally best-selling author with *You Just Don't Understand*: *Women and Men in Conversation*, published by Virago in 1991, and *That's Not What I Meant*: *How Conversational Style Makes or Breaks Your Relations With Others*, published by Virago in 1992. She is one of three University Professors at Georgetown University, Washington, DC – and the only woman of the three. She is a Fellow at the Center for Advanced Study in the Behavioral Sciences at Stanford, California, for the academic year 1992–93. Her permanent home is Washington, DC.

When Virago told me about their twentieth birthday Keepsake, I knew I wanted to be part of it. I could still recall my excitement when I read, twenty years ago, of the establishment of a woman-run publishing company in Britain, and my pleasure when I learned, years later, that Virago would be my British publisher for *You Just Don't Understand: Women and Men in Conversation*.

The obvious choice for the Keepsake was an opinion piece I had just completed for *The New York Times* about Hillary Clinton. The treatment she received from the American press during the 1992 presidential campaign, which was in full swing in the United States, provided a vivid and chilling contemporary example of the double bind in which all women find themselves — a double bind I had described in *You Just Don't Understand*.

Bill Clinton has now been elected president. The knowledge that Hillary Rodham Clinton will be what Americans call The First Lady gives American women hope and pride, just as the creation of Virago gave hope and pride to women in the UK.

My brief essay was rather heavily edited and shortened by *The New York Times*. I am pleased to offer it here in its original form, slightly modified for British readers.

Deborah Tannen
Stanford, California
December, 1992

THE REAL HILLARY FACTOR
by DEBORAH TANNEN

I was a guest on a radio talk show discussing how women's and men's differing conversational styles could lead to misunderstandings, when a man called in to say that he and his wife got along very well because they agreed there could be only one boss in the house, and he was it. The talk show host, a woman, responded at length that she didn't see why anyone had to be boss: relationships are, after all, a partnership. When he needs something, she should listen; when she needs something, he should listen. Both should share equally in resources and rights. When she was done, pleased with the self-evident rightness and clarity of her statement, she took another call. It was a man who said, 'That's what's wrong with you women. You want to dominate us.' The host said, 'Excuse me for a moment. I'm going to scream.' And then she did, right into the microphone: long, high-pitched and wordless.

It was a scream of frustration and bewilderment. It was a scream about the Hillary Factor.

The Hillary Factor, when the phrase was coined in the who's-winning-who's-losing frame through which American presidential elections are reported, referred to the question: Will Hillary Clinton help or hinder her husband's chances to win? But the real Hillary Factor is the double bind that affects all successful or accomplished women – indeed, all women who do not fit stereotypical images of self-deprecatory femininity and all women who do: a woman who is not clearly submissive in her manner is seen as dominating, and is reviled for it. If she does fit the image, she isn't taken seriously. Like Hillary Clinton, women are damned-if-you-do, damned-if-you-don't.

When the Clintons protected their daughter by keeping her away from campaign publicity, polls showed that people thought they were childless, a damning aberration for which the wife is held responsible. When evidence accrued that Hillary Clinton was a devoted mother, *Time* magazine found her guilty of 'yuppie overdoting on her daughter'. No woman can escape the Motherhood Bind: if you're not a Mother, you're a Failed Woman. If you are a Mother, you can't have enough attention to pay to serious work. If you are paying attention to serious work, you must be a Bad Mother.

A woman can't win the Appearance Bind either. When Hillary Clinton wore a homey, unpretentious headband, her hair was called harsh and 'lifelessly doll-like'. When she got a more modish hairstyle, she was accused of modifying her image for political purposes. Wherever she stood, the cameras found her and the headlines yelled that she 'grabbed' the spotlight.

We heard Hillary Clinton called a 'hardheaded careerist'. What, exactly, is a 'careerist'? On the model of 'sexist', is it someone who discriminates on the basis of careers? Or, like 'feminist', is it someone who supports the rights of careers? Or is it just a word, meaningless in itself, that brings to mind the negative image of a woman who has one – negative simply because she is female and works in a profession in which she demonstrates commitment and expertise, rather than a job she doesn't care that much about?

Hillary Clinton was also called humourless, though her friends insist she has a terrific sense of humour. A man is not expected to smile and laugh his way through a speech. But women are expected to laugh and smile frequently, and most do. In social settings, laughing and smiling can be 'don't take me too seriously' signs of harmlessness that put others at ease, but if women talking about serious matters smile and laugh frequently, they look silly. If they don't, they are scorned as 'humourless' (read 'unfeminine').

I live with the Hillary Factor. I have often been told at academic conferences, 'Gee, you're nothing like what I expected. You're softer and nicer.' I ask, 'What made you think I'd be anything else?' The answer: 'Because you've published so much.' A woman who succeeds, they seem to assume, must be tough and mean – unfeminine and unlikeable.

It is reassuring that Republicans failed to make Bill Clinton's wife into what a *Time* writer called 'Willary Horton', alluding to the black convict whose scary image Republicans used to defeat Democratic candidate Michael Dukakis in 1988. But it is instructive that the attempt was made. It forced us to ask, by what logic could it be scary rather than comforting for the wife of a president, whom everyone knows will have his ear, to be unusually intelligent, knowledgeable and accomplished? And to answer: by no logic at all, but by the emotions – fear and anger – that confront women who don't conform to stereotypical expectations. Though the Hillary Factor has apparently been laid to rest in the presidential campaign, it is good to have a name for the kinds of binds that women will be grappling with for a long time to come.

October 1992

BARBARA TAYLOR

was born in western Canada in 1950. She moved to London as a postgraduate student in 1971, studying at the London School of Economics until 1974 and the University of Sussex, where she completed her doctoral dissertation in 1980. This was published by Virago in 1983 as *Eve and the New Jerusalem: Socialism and Feminism in the Nineteenth Century* and was awarded the Isaac Deutscher Memorial Prize in 1984. She has been a lecturer in adult and higher education, is an editor of *History Workshop Journal* and has written two children's books. She is currently working on a study of Mary Wollstonecraft's feminism, to be published by Virago, and lives in London.

MAKING HISTORY:
THE VIRAGO REPRINT LIBRARY

by BARBARA TAYLOR

I think it was 1975 when I went to Carmen Callil's tiny flat in Chelsea. Someone had told Ursula Owen about my doctoral dissertation on early socialist feminism and I'd received a letter: did I want to meet to discuss turning my thesis into a book to be published by a new feminist publishing house, Virago? Yes, I did; and so there I was, surrounded by a lot of emerald green (walls? carpet?) and being investigated by some very white, intimidating cats. There was a little room which represented the entire offices of Virago and the whole staff was there – Carmen and Ursula. The enterprise seemed grandiose, fantastic – almost as fantastic as my own hopes of writing a book for them to publish. But what the hell – I signed the contract. Eight years later Virago brought out my *Eve and the New Jerusalem*. It got great reviews and I became the first woman to receive the Isaac Deutscher Memorial Prize. I'm not sure of the point of this story, except that I like the image of the three of us sitting there in the mid-seventies surrounded by papers and cats, full of ambitions so startlingly realised.

I was brought into women's history by Sally Alexander, Sheila Rowbotham and Anna Davin. Sheila's early books,

Hidden from History (1973) and *Women, Resistance and Revolution* (1972), rescued me from a dreary dissertation on John Dewey, and they became my Bible. Sheila had also published a pamphlet bibliography of women's history, and I set myself to read most of the items on it. It was in this way that I was introduced to an older generation of feminist scholars – Alice Clark, Ivy Pinchbeck, Isabella O'Malley. I read their books in the British Museum and then scoured second-hand bookshops for them. Pinchbeck's *Women Workers and the Industrial Revolution, 1750–1850* (1930, reprinted by Virago in 1981) I eventually knew almost by heart; I have memories of arguing over her interpretation of women's economic role in my study group on the Family and Industrialisation in about 1977. It was around that time also that Sally Alexander and I began co-teaching classes in women's history and feminist theory, and then I met a host of other predecessors – feminist radicals like Ray Strachey, Sylvia Pankhurst, Maud Pember Reeves. Sally's affectionately acute understanding of these women – partly captured in her excellent introduction to the Virago reprint of Maud Pember Reeves's *Round About a Pound a Week* – probably taught me more about late nineteenth/early twentieth-century feminism than anything else before or since.

Round About a Pound a Week – Pember Reeves's 1913 portrait of the lives of the Lambeth working poor – was one of the first of the Virago historical reprints, preceded by Margaret Llewelyn Davies's 1931 *Life as We Have Known It* (introduced by Anna Davin) and followed by about a dozen more, mostly authored by women who had been in or around the turn-of-the-century Left. In her introduction to the reprint of Clementina Black's 1915 *Married Women's Work*, Ellen Mappen described these left-wing women as 'social feminists', meaning women who 'connected social reform with obtaining women's rights':

> Some, but not all, were socialists. Many were also active in the suffrage movement but at the same time they did not allow other women's issues to be ignored by the general public or by government officials. The groups they formed, which included the [Women's Industrial] Council, the Women's Co-operative Guild, the Women's Labour League, and the Fabian Women's Group, became an informal but wide-ranging network of women committed to ameliorating women's position in society.

These women were all products of the most reform-minded wing of the Victorian and Edwardian middle class, imbued with the fierce intellectualism and philanthropic zeal so characteristic of that grouping. Despite these class origins, however, they were anything but 'bourgeois feminists', being deeply committed to creating a feminist politics which would transcend class differences. Indeed, it was the condition of working-class women, the poorest of their sisters, which many of them saw as an index for female advancement in general. 'We read about [the working class] and talk about them, and tabulate what qualities are needed to make those lives satisfactory . . . until their vices and virtues seem to have become a sort of standard currency of ethics: and especially as regards women,' Lady Florence Bell wrote (herself the author of the 1907 study of the Middlesbrough working class, *At the Works*, also reprinted by Virago).

Drawing on the traditions of Victorian social explorers, these women – particularly Fabian women – went into working-class districts to meet female inhabitants, document their lives, and assist in the growth of their industrial and political organisations. The ideology that infused all this, as Sally Alexander describes, was economic individualism: women of all classes must be assisted to achieve economic independence from men and, on that basis, to become equal citizens. 'To study the economic position of women and press their claim to equality with men in the personal economic independence to be secured by socialism' was the first aim of the Fabian Women's Group in 1913. (An earlier report of the group reminded its members that such aims required them to 'cast aside feminine slackness and negligence with regard to their own affairs' – a feminist puritanism which still had plenty of echoes in the 1970s.)

These were the economic and political ambitions which inspired not only feminist social investigations like that of Bell or Llewelyn Davies or Pember Reeves, but also such important works of feminist scholarship as Pinchbeck's book, or Barbara Drake's 1920 *Women and Trade Unions*, or Ray Strachey's 1928 history of feminism, *The Cause* – all also reprinted by Virago. In bringing the writings of these women back to life, then, Virago has provided essential resources for the student of women's history – but more, it has given us a window into the mental world of an earlier feminist generation. Documenting the history of the women's rights movement in England up to enfranchisement, Ray Strachey wrote: 'I feel bound to confess at the outset that in writing this book I have not been unbiased. I was myself an actor in the later stages of the Suffrage drama, and thus I am both open to and proud of the charge that I cannot take a wholly impartial view.' It is precisely for this engaged and 'partial' view of the lives, hopes and struggles of nineteenth- and early twentieth-century women that we now so much value the writings of these earlier feminist activists and intellectuals – and applaud Virago (and the authors of the reprints' fine introductions) for keeping them alive and available to us.

TATYANA TOLSTAYA

was born in what was then the Soviet Union in 1951, a relative of Leo Tolstoy, and granddaughter of Alexei Tolstoy. She worked for several years in a Moscow publishing house. Her first collection of stories, *On the Golden Porch*, was published in the Soviet Union in 1987, and was sold out of bookshops within the hour. Virago published it to enormous acclaim in 1989, and in 1992 her second collection, *Sleepwalker in a Fog*. She has taught at universities in Texas and Virgina, and currently divides her time between Moscow and Princetown University, where she is a Visiting Research Fellow.

FROM: A SHORT TOUR OF THE RUSSIAN ASYLUM

by TATYANA TOLSTAYA
translated by FRANCECSA NICOLAS

S omeone recently made the witty observation that Russia is a country whose past cannot be predicted. This is very true, and it is very convenient. Everyone dreams up their own past, their own history of this lunatic asylum, and no one story is any better or any more accurate than another. There are as many pasts as you could wish for. Is this not the highest freedom, the highest form of equality? And is it not the best and most fertile soil for literature?

And since there is nowhere to go and no reason to move, and time has no length and no direction, then any grumbles about Russia (that it has, as they say, conquered half the world, subjected and oppressed innumerable nations, is guilty of economic stagnation, has broken up the cultures of subject races and, indeed, its own) are, from a Russian point of view, groundless, since they are merely relative. What grounds for complaint can there be? Einstein has explained it all, hasn't he? It is only from your point of view, the point of view of an outside observer, that Russia has· spread from ocean to ocean, for, with your linear western logic, you believe in different sides of the world, in the wind rose, in atmospheric pressure, in miles and in kilometres. But from the Russian point of view we are *here*. If we go a thousand miles away, we will again be *here*. We do not believe in arithmetic. Wherever we are, that is *here*. So does it really matter where we are? . . .

It is equally meaningless to talk of stagnation, for we live *now*, and stagnation is a process, and we do not understand processes. Meaningless, too, to talk of destruction, of the demolition, for instance, of some beautiful church. *Yesterday* it was there, *today* it is not. But, you see, one can put it the other way round. *Today* it is not there, *yesterday* it was. And *the day before yesterday* it was again not there. So it follows that *the day before yesterday* is no different from *today*, while *yesterday* is merely a transient ripple, a whim – it ruffled the surface and is gone. Perhaps it will ruffle the surface again. 'Perhaps' ('maybe') is a favourite Russian word, neither yes nor no, neither to the right nor to the left, neither forwards nor backwards.

All over the world people re-set their clocks twice a year, changing from summer time to winter time. A saving is made on electricity, and it is, is it not, somehow more pleasant, more natural to sleep in the dark and go out in the sunlight. In Russia they also play about with the clocks, but not from economic considerations, not for convenience, but . . . just like that, for no particular reason. Once, when Stalin was still alive, they *forgot* to re-set the clocks at the right moment, and when they remembered they were afraid to tell Stalin. He did not notice, so life went on like that – right up to this year, even though Stalin died forty years ago, so there was no one to be afraid of any more. A population of 250 million, 150 million Russians – and none of them cared.

ANGELA CARTER

was born in 1940 and lived in Yorkshire, Bristol, Japan and
south London. Her first novel, *Shadow Dance*, appeared in
1965. She won the 1967 John Llewellyn Rhys Prize for *The
Magic Toyshop* and the 1968 Somerset Maugham Award
for *Several Perceptions*. These were followed by short story
collections and novels, along with much lively journalism,
collected in *Nothing Sacred* (Virago, 1982) and *Expletives
Deleted* (Chatto & Windus, 1992) and three anthologies for
Virago: *Wayward Girls and Wicked Women* (1986), *The
Virago Book of Fairy Tales* (1990) and *The Second Virago
Book of Fairy Tales* (1992). She wrote the film scripts for
The Company of Wolves and *The Magic Toyshop*. She died
in February 1992.

Marina Warner is a novelist, a critic and the author of
distinguished studies of cultural myths and symbols. Her
latest novel, *Indigo*, appeared in 1992, and a collection
of short stories, *The Mermaids in the Basement*, was
published this year.

PUBLISHER'S NOTE
We are grateful to Marina Warner for permission to
include this extract from her Introduction to Angela
Carter's *Second Virago Book of Fairy Tales*. It appears
in memory of Angela Carter, to show our gratitude for the
unstinting support and friendship she gave us at Virago.

ANGELA CARTER: HEROIC OPTIMISM, FANTASTIC FLIGHTS*

by MARINA WARNER

I talo Calvino, the Italian writer and fabulist and collector of fairy tales, believed strongly in the connection between fantasy and reality: 'I am accustomed to consider literature a search for knowledge,' he wrote. 'Faced with [the] precarious existence of tribal life, the shaman responded by ridding his body of weight and flying to another world, another level of perception, where he could find the strength to change the face of reality.'[1] Angela Carter wouldn't have made the same wish with quite such a straight face, but her combination of fantasy and revolutionary longings corresponds to the flight of Calvino's shaman. She possessed the enchanter's lightness of mind and wit – it's interesting that she explored, in her last two novels, images of winged women. Fevvers, her aërialiste heroine of *Nights at the Circus*, may have hatched like a bird, and in *Wise Children*, the twin Chance sisters play various fairies or feathered creatures, from their first foot on the stage as child stars to their dalliance in Hollywood for a spectacular extravaganza of *A Midsummer Night's Dream*.

Fairy tales also offered her a means of flying – of finding and telling an alternative story, of shifting something in the mind, just as so many fairy-tale characters shift something in their shape. She wrote her own – the dazzling, erotic variations on Perrault's Mother Goose tales and other familiar stories in *The Bloody Chamber* – and she lifted Beauty and Red Riding Hood and Bluebeard's last wife out of the pastel nursery into the labyrinth of female desire. She had always read very widely in folklore from all over the world, and compiled her first collection, *The Virago Book of Fairy Tales*, three years ago; the second volume was published after her death in February 1992 from cancer.

She found the stories in sources ranging from Siberia to Surinam, and she arranged them into sections in a sequence that runs from one tale of female heroic endeavour to another about generosity rewarded. There are few fairies, in the sense of sprites, but the stories move in fairyland, not the prettified, kitschified, Victorians' elfland, but the darker, dream realm of spirits and tricks, magical, talking animals, riddles and spells. In 'The Twelve Wild Ducks', the opening tale, the heroine vows not to speak or to laugh or to cry until she has rescued her brothers from their enchanted animal forms. The issue of women's speech, of women's noise, of their/our clamour and laughter and weeping and shouting and hooting runs through all Angela Carter's writings, and informed her love of the folk tale. In *The Magic Toyshop* the lovely Aunt Margaret cannot speak because she is strangled by the silver torque which the malign puppetmaster her husband has made her as a bridal gift . . .

Angela Carter's partisan feeling for women, which burns in all her work, never led her to any conventional form of feminism; but she continues here one of her original and effective strategies, snatching, out of the jaws of misogyny itself, 'useful stories' for women. Her essay 'The Sadeian Woman' (1979) found in Sade a liberating teacher of the male—female status quo and made him illuminate the farther reaches of women's polymorphous desires; here she turns topsy-turvy some cautionary folk tales and shakes out the fear and dislike of women they once expressed to create a new set of values, about strong, outspoken, zestful, sexual women who can't be kept down. In *Wise Children*, she created a heroine, Dora Chance, who's a showgirl, a soubrette, a vaudeville dancer, one of the low, the despised, the invisible poor, an old woman who's illegitimate and never married (born the wrong side of the blanket, the wrong side of the tracks), and each of these stigmas is taken up with exuberant relish and scattered in the air like so much wedding confetti.

The last story, 'Spreading the Fingers', a tough morality tale from Surinam about sharing what one has been given with others, also discloses the high value Angela Carter placed on generosity. She gave of herself – her ideas, her wit, her incisive, no-bullshit mind – with open but never sentimental prodigality. Her favourite fairy tale in the first *Virago Book* was a Russian riddle story 'The Wise Little Girl', in which the tsar asks her heroine for the impossible, and she delivers it without batting an eyelid. Angela liked it because it was as satisfying as 'The Emperor's New Clothes', but 'no one was humiliated and everybody gets the prizes'. The story comes in the section called 'Clever Women, Resourceful Girls and Desperate Stratagems', and its heroine is an essential Carter figure, never abashed, nothing daunted, sharp-eared as a vixen and possessed of dry good sense. It's entirely characteristic of Angela's spirit that she should delight in the tsar's confounding, and yet not want him to be humiliated.

She did not have the strength, before she died, to write the introduction she had planned to this volume, but she left four cryptic notes among her papers:

'every real story contains something useful, says Walter Benjamin

the *unperplexedness* of the story

"No one dies so poor that he does not leave something behind," said Pascal.

Fairy tales – cunning and high spirits'.

Fragmentary as they are, these phrases convey the Carter philosophy. She was scathing about the contempt the 'educated' can show, when two-thirds of the literature of the world – perhaps more – has been created by the illiterate. She liked the solid common sense of folk tales, the straightforward aims of their protagonists, the simple moral distinctions, and the wily stratagems they suggest. They're tales of the underdog, about cunning and high spirits winning through in the end; they're practical, and they're not high-flown. For a fantasist with wings, Angela kept her eyes on the ground, with reality firmly in her sights. She once remarked, 'A fairy tale is a story where one king goes to another king to borrow a cup of sugar.'

Feminist critics of the genre – especially in the 1970s – jibbed at the socially conventional 'happy endings' of so many stories (for example, 'When she grew up he married her and she became the tsarina'). But Angela knew about satisfaction and pleasure; and at the same time she believed that the goal of fairy tales wasn't 'a conservative one, but a utopian one, indeed a form of heroic optimism – as if to say: One day, we might be happy even if it won't last.' Her own heroic optimism never failed her – like the spirited heroine of one of her tales, she was resourceful and brave and even funny during the illness which brought about her death. Few writers possess the best qualities of their work; she did, in spades.

Her imagination was dazzling, and through her daring, vertiginous plots, her precise yet wild imagery, her gallery of wonderful bad-good girls, beasts, rogues and other creatures, she causes readers to hold their breath as a mood of heroic optimism forms against the odds. She had the true writer's gift of remaking the world for her readers.

She was a wise child herself, with a mobile face, a mouth which sometimes pursed with irony, and, behind the glasses, a wryness, at times a twinkle, at times a certain dreaminess; with her long, silvery hair and ethereal delivery, she had something of the Faerie Queene about her, except that she was never wispy or fey. And though the narcissism of youth was one of the great themes in her early fiction, she was herself exceptionally un-narcissistic. Her voice was soft, with a storyteller's confidingness, and lively with humour; she spoke with a certain syncopation, as she stopped to think – her thoughts made her the most exhilarating companion, a wonderful talker, who wore her learning and wide reading with lightness, who could express a mischievous insight or a tough judgement with scalpel precision and produce new ideas by the dozen without effort, weaving allusion, quotation, parody and original invention, in a way that echoed her prose style. 'I've got a theory that . . .' she'd say, self-deprecatorily, and then would follow something that no one else had thought of, some sally, some rich paradox that would encapsulate a trend, a moment. She could be Wildean in her quickness and the glancing drollery of her wit. And then she would pass on, sometimes leaving her listeners astonished and stumbling.

NOTES

* This introduction contains material from Marina Warner's obituary of Angela Carter which appeared in the *Independent* 18 February 1992.

1. Italo Calvino, *Six Memos for the Next Millennium*, trans. William Weaver, London, 1992, p. 26.

ELIZABETH WILSON

is Professor in the Department of Environmental and Social Studies at the University of North London. She has long been involved in the women's movement, the lesbian and gay movement and in left politics. She is the author of a number of books, including *Adorned in Dreams* (Virago, 1985) and *The Sphinx in the City*, (Virago, 1991), and contributes to the *Gaurdian* and *New Statesman and Society*. She lives in London with her partner and daughter.

KNITTING

by ELIZABETH WILSON

I first met Carmen Callil and Ursula Owen in I forget which year, but it would have to have been 1973 or 1974. It was at a women's meeting – of course, where else. I spent my whole life at women's meetings. Strangely enough, I did have a full-time job, but my memory of it is eclipsed by the intensity of political life; in fact I was totally out of touch with most of my colleagues and students, blindly imagining that they were as obsessed with politics as I. The women's movement and 'the left' was the element in which I swam, and, to paraphrase the poet Shelley, 'like a dome of many-coloured glass' it stained the grey dreariness of life in crisis-of-capitalism Britain.

At this particular meeting Carmen, like me, was knitting. Knitting – having been, for this segment of the sixties generation, a dismal emblem of domestic servitude and sexless femininity – was having a revival, re-evaluated as an underrated women's craft. Where once any independent career woman would have spurned it, we now began to see its beauty and interest. The concept of career woman was, in any case, no part of feminist ideology, although we campaigned for the right to work. I see us now as closer to the women of the Aesthetic movement in the 1890s, who wore 'socialist gowns', left off their corsets and cut their hair. This side of the 1970s women's movement has been forgotten or denied. The ugly stereotype of 'harridans in dungarees' is worse than merely inaccurate or sexist, for it effaces the desire for a harmonious life which underlay the whole atmosphere of 'struggle' in which the women's movement was also steeped. We wanted work and home life, child care and other forms of creative endeavour to be integrated instead of parcelled up into separate times and places. Personal appearance and the kinds of interior in which this life was to be lived were equally the focus of feminist attention. In this, again, the feminist movement of the 1970s resembled nineteenth-century utopianism in its wish to create a total world, an aspiration little understood by the conservative feminism of the 1980s. An interest in crafts and the conservation and appreciation of second-hand clothes and furniture was an important element in this vision. It could be anti-consumerist without being puritanical, or rather could acknowledge that consumerism as a love of beautiful objects need not be wasteful.

My knitted jumpers in – I thought, anyway – subtle colours and patterns expressed this aesthetic, and self-adornment could become what almost amounted to the wearing of a work of art: uniqueness without excessive individualism, beauty without undue display.

Knitting was also a soothing occupation in meetings when feelings tended to run high.

That meeting, at which I met Carmen, knitting like me, was the occasion on which I first heard about Virago. I am sure I could not have guessed how important it would become to the women's movement, and to me.

I wonder if Carmen still knits? I do not – and this is mysterious to me. Somehow the 1980s were not conducive to knitting. The soft Liberty colours did not go with the new decade. Now career women were everywhere, and bulky jackets replaced the 'period' jumpers, blouses and frocks.

My friend Mary once said that my handwriting was like knitting, all joined up in every direction. I wrote so much in the eighties; perhaps that was my knitting – a word misplaced, like a dropped stitch, and the whole thing can unravel, but when it goes right you feel pleased in much the same way.

Knitting had that extra something, though – a tangible object, a garment useful and beautiful. I would love the same to be said of my books – but are they warm and comforting too? I fear not. Knitting expressed a straightforward love of colour and pattern; for my books are reserved all the ambiguities of life.

VIRAGO BOOKS BY THE
KEEPSAKE AUTHORS

MAYA ANGELOU
I Know Why the Caged
  Bird Sings 0 86068 511 X
  WXUSAC
Gather Together in My Name
  0 86068 685 X WXUSAC
Singin' and Swingin' and
  Gettin' Merry Like
  Christmas 0 86068 673 6
WXUSAC
The Heart of a Woman
  0 86068 678 7 WXUSAC
All God's Children Need
  Travelling Shoes 0 86068
  907 7 WXUSAC
Maya Angelou Omnibus
  1 85381 455 5 WXUSAC
Conversations With Maya
  Angelou ed. J. Elliott
  1 85381 107 6 WXUSAC

MARGARET ATWOOD
Bluebeard's Egg 0 86068
996 4 WXUSAC
Bodily Harm 0 86068 344 3
  WXUSAC
Cat's Eye 1 85381 126 2
  WXUSAC

Dancing Girls 0 86068 456 3
  WXUSAC
The Edible Woman 0 86068
  129 7 WXUSAC
The Handmaid's Tale 0 86068
  866 6 WXUSAC
Lady Oracle 0 86068 303 6
  WXUSAC
Life Before Man 0 86068 1920
  WXUSAC
Surfacing 0 86068 064 9
  WXUSAC
Wilderness Tips 1 85381 3958
  WXUSAC
Atwood: Conversations ed.
  Earl Ingersoll 1 85381 511X
  WXUSAC

NINA BAWDEN
Birds on the Trees 1 85381
  373 7 W
Family Money 1 85381 486 5
  WXUSA
The Ice House 1 85381
  434 2 W
A Little Love, A Little
  Learning 1 85381
  006 1 W

117

Tortoise by Candlelight
1 85381 005 3
Walking Naked 1 85381
444 X W
A Woman of My Age 1 85381
322 2 W

ANGELA CARTER
Fireworks 0 86068 402 4
WXUSAC
The Magic Toyshop 0 86068
190 4 WXUSAC
The Passion of New Eve
086068 341 9 WXUSA
The Sadeian Woman: An
Exercise in Cultural History
0 86068 055 X WXUSA
Wayward Girls and Wicked
Women 0 86068 579 9
WXUSA
The Virago Book of Fairy
Tales hbk 1 85381 205 6;
pbk 1 85381 440 7
WXUSA
The Second Virago Book of
Fairy Tales 1 85381 491 1
WXUSA

WILLA CATHER
Alexander's Bridge 1 85381
163 7 WXUSAC
Death Comes for the
Archbishop 0 86068 183 1
WXUSAC
A Lost Lady 0 8668 126 2
WXUSAC
Lucy Gayheart 0 86068 512 8
WXUSAC
My Antonia 0 86068 125 4
WXUSAC
My Mortal Enemy 0 86068
246 3 WXUSAC

One of Ours 0 86068 502 0
WXUSAC
O Pioneers! 0 86068 310 9
WXUSAC
The Professor's House 0
86068 184 X WXUSAC
Sapphira and the Slave Girl 0
86068 507 1 WXUSAC
The Short Stories of Willa
Cather 1 85381 108 4
WXUSAC
The Song of the Lark 0 86068
245 5 WXUSAC

AMANDA CROSS
A Death in the Faculty
0 86068 896 8 WXUSAC
In the Last Analysis 1 85381
488 1 WXUSAC
The James Joyce Murder
0 86068 074 6 WXUSAC
No Word From Winifred
0 86068 853 4 WXUSAC
The Players Come Again 1
85381 515 2 WXUSAC
Poetic Justice 1 85381 025 8
WXUSAC
A Question of Max 0 86068
107 6 WXUSAC
Sweet Death, Kind Death 0
86068 483 0 WXUSAC
The Theban Mysteries 1
85381 024 X WXUSAC
A Trap for Fools 1 85381
093 2 WXUSAC

KATHLEEN DAYUS
All My Days 0 86068
076 2 W
Her People 0 86068 275 7 W
Where There's Life 0 86068
623 X W

Best of Times 1 85381
376 1 W
The People of Lavender Court
1 85381 626 4 W

**JANETTE TURNER
HOSPITAL**
Borderline 1 85381 160 2
WXUSACNZ
Charades 1 85381 169 6
WXUSACNZ
Isobars 1 85381 509 8
WXUSACNZ
The Last Magician hbk
1 85381 325 7; pbk 185381
605 1 WXUSACANZ
The Tiger in the Tiger
Pit 1 85381 225 0
WXUSACNZ

ALICE MILLER
Banished Knowledge:
*Facing Childhood
Injuries* 1 85381 154 8
Breaking Down the
Wall of Silence hbk
1 85381 461 X
pbk 1 85381 473 3
WXUSAC
The Drama of Being a
Child 0 86068 898 4
WXUSAC
For Your Own Good: *The
Roots of Violence in
Child Rearing*
0 86068 899 2 WXUSAC
The Untouched Key:
*Tracing Childhood
Trauma in Creativity and
Destructiveness* 1 85381
187 4 WXUSAC

KATE MILLETT
The Loony Bin Trip 1 85381
326 5 WXUSAC
Sexual Politics 0 86068 029 0
WXUSAC

GRACE NICHOLS
The Fat Black Woman's Poems
0 86068 635 3 W
Lazy Thoughts of a Lazy
Woman 1 85381 076 2 W

MICHÈLE ROBERTS
Daughters of the House hbk
1 85381 550 0; pbk 185381
600 0 WXUSA

LYNNE SEGAL
Is the Future Female? 0 86068
697 3 WXUSA
Sex Exposed: *Sexuality and
the Pornography Debate*
1 85381 385 0 WXUSAC
Slow Motion: *Changing
Masculinities, Changing
Men* 1 85381 013 4
WXUSA

ELAINE SHOWALTER
The Female Malady:
*Women, Madness
and English Culture
1830–1980*
0 86068 869 0 WXUSAC
A Literature of Their Own:
*Women Writers from
Charlotte Brontë to Doris
Lessing* 0 86068 285 4
WXUSAC
New Feminist Criticism
0 86068 727 9 WXUSAC

Sexual Anarchy: *Gender and Culture at the Fin de Siècle* 1 85381 277 3 WXUSAC

GILLIAN SLOVO
Betrayal 1 85381 475 X WXUSA

DEBORAH TANNEN
That's Not What I Meant 1 85381 512 8 WXUSAC
You Just Don't Understand 1 85381 471 7 WXUSAC

BARBARA TAYLOR
Eve and the New Jerusalem 0 86068 258 7 WXUSA

TATYANA TOLSTAYA
On the Golden Porch 1 85381 078 9 WXUSAC
Sleepwalker in a Fog 1 85381 305 2 WXUSAC

THE VIRAGO REPRINT LIBRARY
At the Works, Lady Florence Bell 0 86068 415 6 W
The Cause, Ray Strachey 0 86068 042 8 W
Life as We Have Known It, Margaret Llewelyn Davies 0 86068 000 2 W
Married Women's Work, Clementina Black 0 86068 410 5 W
Round About a Pound a Week, Pember Reeves 0 86068 066 5 W

Women and Trade Unions, Barbara Drake 0 86068 405 9 W
Women Workers and the Industrial Revolution, 1750–1850, Ivy Pinchbeck 0 86068 170 X W

ELIZABETH WILSON
Adorned in Dreams 0 86068 557 8 WXUSA
The Lost Time Café 1 85381 611 6 WXUSA
The Sphinx in the City 1 85381 282 X WXUSA

ANTONIA WHITE
As Once in May 0 86068 357 5 W
Beyond the Glass 0 86068 097 5 W
Frost in May 0 86068 049 5 W
The Lost Traveller 0 86068 095 9 W
Minka and Curdy 1 85381 552 7 W
Strangers 0 86068 171 8 W
The Sugar House 0 86068 096 7 W
Antonia White Diaries 1926–1957 ed. Susan Chitty 1 85381 489 X WXUSAC
Antonia White Diaries 1958–1979 ed. Susan Chitty 1 85381 631 0 WXUSAC